You Have a New Friend Request

Do You accept?

Brent M. Craine

WESTBOW
PRESS®
A DIVISION OF THOMAS NELSON
& ZONDERVAN

WestBow Press books may be ordered through booksellers or by contacting:

WestBow Press
A Division of Thomas Nelson & Zondervan
1663 Liberty Drive
Bloomington, IN 47403
www.westbowpress.com
1 (866) 928-1240

ISBN: 978-1-5127-6530-4 (sc)
ISBN: 978-1-5127-6531-1 (hc)
ISBN: 978-1-5127-6529-8 (e)

Library of Congress Control Number: 2016919393

Print information available on the last page.

WestBow Press rev. date: 11/29/2016

Introduction

This collection of reflections is one year of postings on Facebook, and it is the result of prayer and the desire to help people be comfortable with the word of God. These ruminations are the result of giving up Facebook during Lent. I spent a lot of time during the day watching what everyone else was doing with their lives and talking about my political ideas. No single idea in politics is acceptable by all people, so I would occasionally make people mad with my thoughts and ideas. I started to realize that this was not healthy for me, and it wasn't what I would call a healthy habit. Because I gave up Facebook for Lent, I spent a lot of time in prayer and trying to understand what this sacrifice was going to do for me. The more I prayed about it, the more I heard God telling me that I could use Facebook for good. Most people who are on Facebook are not looking for any one thing in particular; they are just looking. I started with posting scripture passages from my daily Catholic Mass readings. I then tried experimenting with sharing my thoughts while I read these passages. Most are not necessarily theological thoughts, but things that God has put into my heart and head to think about. After getting a few likes and comments, I thought maybe this wasn't getting the response I had hoped for, so I decided to stop posting, and then it started. People started private messaging me and saying they were reading my posts every day. I had no idea because, as I said, I had only a few likes and comments on my posts. Then I had people that were on my friends list, who I never expected to read my reflections, telling me that they read them but never clicked on "like" because they were the type who never let people know they were on Facebook.

At this point I realized that not everyone on Facebook clicks on like, makes a comment, or shares when they like something, especially when it is something they fear other people will judge them for. Some of the people that have been reading my reflections on a regular basis were not necessarily religious or spiritual people, but they like the questions that were asked, and thus were drawn in.

While reading these reflections, remember that these are done each morning, and sometimes the scripture is repeated during the year. Also remember that I am not an ordained religious person, only a layperson, like yourself, trying to make a difference. I have taught catechism since 1991, and I have learned that people do not always attend church because they don't hear what they want to hear, or what they need to hear. I have left the content the same as it appeared on my Facebook page to maintain the original thoughts. I did, however, make some grammatical corrections. Most of these were written on my Kindle while lying in bed, before I got up to start my day. My goal is to make people want to learn more about what God can do in their lives, and want to spend more time in God's word. My hope and prayer is that God uses me to reach people who may not actively seek inspiration but need it in their lives, just like you and me. Although I am a Catholic Christian, there are a lot of thoughts that all Christians can reflect on. I have even had some agnostic and atheist friends read them, and it stirred them to ask questions.

I have posted the scripture reference at the end of each day that helped to instigate the reflection. The scripture passages are from the Catholic Mass reading for each day during the year 2015. There are a few days that are missing, and I apologize for that, as there is no real easy way to go back that far on Facebook to retrieve them.

The Spirit of the Lord is upon me, because he has anointed me to bring glad tidings to the poor. He has sent me to proclaim liberty to captives and recovery of sight to the blind, to let the oppressed go free, and to proclaim a year acceptable to the Lord.(Luke 4: 18–19)

January 1, 2015

Do you take the time to bless people in God's name? How do you bless them? In this reading from the book of Numbers, we see God teaching Moses how to rain down God's blessings on his people. Will you take the time to ask for God's blessings on the people you come in contact with? Let God's words be your words for this New Year. Happy New Year, and may the Lord bless you and keep you. May the Lord let his face shine on you and be gracious to you. May the Lord uncover his face to you and bring you peace.

Lord, may I be not so much a seeker of your blessings as a giver of your blessings.

Numbers 6:22–27

January 2, 2015

How hard is it to profess your faith when you are asked what you believe? Do you ever have to pause because you're not sure if you will offend someone? Or what if they don't agree with you, and you have to defend your faith in Jesus Christ? Who would you rather offend—God our Father, or the person you are being questioned by? There are greater consequences for offending God than a relationship with that person. These are challenging questions, so please pray about them.

Lord, you know my heart, and you know my human weaknesses. Please grant me the strength to never deny you, no matter who is questioning me.

1 John 2:22–28

January 3, 2015

When you see God in your everyday life, do you recognize him? John the Baptist recognized Jesus because he spent time in prayer, and God told him what to look for in order to know he was the One. The more we talk to someone, the easier it is to recognize that person. Think about those old friends that you see once in a while. You see something familiar about them, but you're not sure of their names, or how you know them. Then think about the people you see every day. You probably never forget their names. Is God like an old friend, or the person you visit with every day?

In you, Lord, I am made aware of all that you have for me to see. May I always recognize you in all things and in all people.

John 1:29–34

January 4, 2015

Do you have dreams that you remember, other than the ones where you're naked in public? Have you ever wondered what they mean? We have heard a lot about dreams in these latest months of readings. Through dreams the Magi heard about a king being born and were told not to return to Jerusalem. They trusted that what they heard was from God, and had the rare pleasure of seeing God in the face of an infant. Does God speak to us through our dreams? God speaks to us in many ways; we just need to know that it is him.

Lord, help me to know your voice as the sheep know the shepherd's voice.

Matthew 2:1–12

January 6, 2015

Have you ever fixed a meal for yourself, and someone shows up right when you're getting ready to eat? Were there leftovers? Jesus never worried about the simple things of this life, like making sure everyone had enough food. He knew due to the love of his Father that all things would be taken care of. Why were there leftovers after all the people were satisfied? Were they all fasting, and people who had extra threw it into the baskets? Maybe God was providing another message. All four Gospels have this same miracle in it, and all have leftover bread and fish. What's the purpose? Is it to show us that we should be fed by God's word, and we will have plenty to share with other people? Was it a sign to take what we have learned and share it? Was this a sign to go out and evangelize? There was more bread and fish left over than what they started out with—does that mean we are not able to contain all of God's word on our own? What do you do with God's word? Do you share it or throw it away?

Lord, may I share your love for me with others, and may I never feel as if I have to keep it to myself.

Mark 6:34–44

January 7, 2015

How often has your life been nearly unbearable and it seems as if nothing will calm it? In those times of desperation, do you complain, or do you take time to pray? The disciples were being tossed about in their boat on the sea from the strong winds, and the winds didn't stop when they saw Jesus walking on the sea. It didn't stop when they acknowledged who he was, either. The winds only died down when Jesus entered their boat. Do you see Jesus, and do you allow him to enter your inner being, or do you merely want to acknowledge who he is? Do you allow him to really enter your life? There is a calmness that you can embrace in knowing you are not in this battle alone, and allowing Jesus to take control of whatever situation you have. Will you ask Jesus to enter your life?

Thank you, Lord, for giving me the peace that you bring, knowing that I am not in this alone. May I always be aware that you are there for me.

Mark 6:45–52

January 8, 2015

Do you have children or siblings? Are you all the same? Do you have a child or sibling that maybe gets into a little more trouble than you or the others? Weren't you all raised by the same parents? How, then, is it the fault of the parent if one gets into more trouble, or does something horrible to someone else? It's not, right? Than how is it that God can be blamed for the wars, and radical people of the world? Just because someone says they are doing something in the name of God, doesn't mean that God approves of it. This letter from John, is what God is trying to teach us, yet we still have people that say, "Religion is the cause of most, if not all, wars". Is that fair? Isn't it usually someone claiming they are doing something in God's name? God has no desire to see the death or destruction of His children, any more than a parent wants to see harm to their children. Do you believe God really wants, what we see happening around the world? Do you love enough to want something different?

Lord, help me to see past the faults of those who want destruction, to love as You love, as a parent loves a child.

1 John 4:19–5:4

January 11, 2015

Why was Jesus baptized? Aren't we baptized for the forgiveness of our sins? Wasn't Jesus without sin? Obviously, He didn't need to be baptized for any reason, other than to show us that it is something we should all do, so that we can wash away our original sin. What does your own baptism mean to you? How about the baptism of your child? Do you think of it as just something to do, or is it something you have to do? Some denominations baptize from birth on, some wait until the person to be baptized is of an age to determine for themselves if they want to be. If we are being baptized to wash away original sin, why wouldn't you baptize as early as possible? Wasn't Jesus' baptism of the Holy Spirit, not to wash away original sin? Does that mean there may be two separate sacraments? Are you baptized? Do you know someone that wants, or needs to be baptized?

Lord, You have given us these sacraments to help us understand Your love for us, may we see them as You meant us to see.

Mark 1:7-11

January 12, 2015

Have you ever wondered why Jesus didn't ask the rich, and people with a known name in society to be his apostles? Do you think maybe He didn't think they would have the stomach, to possibly upset their friends and neighbors, by what He was asking them to do? Maybe He wanted people in the types of professions that knew what it would take, and would be persistent, and determined? Anybody that does a lot of fishing, knows that in order to catch fish, you need to know the fish, and be very persistent to be successful. Didn't He already know what was to be asked of them? Wouldn't He want that kind of character? People that would do whatever it took to be fishers of men. Do you have what it takes to speak to people about their faith? Do you have the persistence to keep going in the face of objection?

Lord You know I am not a good fisherman, but you have taught me what it takes to be a Fisher of men, may I be always faithful, and persistent.

Mark 1:14-20

January 13, 2015

Wait! Before you read this part, read the scripture reading. I need to see if you see what I saw.

Did you happen to notice who said what, in this reading? An unclean spirit, a demon, said, "I know who you are—the Holy One of God!"(Mark 1:24) Are you alright with that? Haven't you heard that, "if you proclaim that Jesus Christ is Lord, with your lips, you will enter the kingdom of heaven!"? Was there Faith in that statement? I think so. Was there love, or works, in that statement? I don't think so. Wouldn't that be a good argument for "Faith and works"? Isn't that a teaching that some Christians will argue? "Faith alone, for salvation." I'm not saying one is right or wrong, I am just saying, there are teachings of the Catholic Church that some people will argue, and this is one of them. Or, is there a demon in Heaven that duped the system? Have you asked God to guide your prayer life, and ask for His vision, and understanding?

Lord, there are so many things that we have done and said that cause us to be conflicted, may Your Holy Spirit guide my thoughts, and words.

Mark 1:21-28

January 14, 2015

Do you volunteer to serve other people, besides your own family members? What if God had touched your life in a special way? Do you feel the need, and the desire to serve then? Simon, who we know as Peter, was one of the apostles that we know was married. When Jesus touched his mother in-laws life, and healed her sickness, she immediately got up and started to serve others. She knew right away something special was going on, and was very grateful for it. Are you grateful for what God has done in your life? What do you do in return? Do you always see the same people at churches and functions, doing the serving? Are they the only ones grateful, because they are old and still alive? Where can you help out?

Lord let me be your servant, that I may serve Your people, as You have served me.

Mark 1:29-39

January 15, 2015

How good are you at keeping a secret? What if it is great news? What if no one would even acknowledge you before the secret, and now you can go anywhere, and be around anyone, and it changed your life, or gave you new life? Would you still be able to keep that secret? Lepers were cast out from all of society, and this man can now associate with people again, and be close to his family again. Would you be silent about that? It is hard to keep a secret that brings you so much joy. Don't you feel like you have to at least tell someone, when you have great news? Would we have known about all the miracles Jesus performed, if the ones He healed were silent? Would He still be changing lives, if they would have kept silent? Do you have a story that has changed your life? Would you share it, if it helped someone else?

Lord, may Your healing power be known to everyone, in whatever it takes to get Your word out.

Mark 1:40-45

January 16, 2015

How good are you at getting to what you want or need? Will you do whatever it takes to get it? What if it was for a friend, more than it was for you? Would you try harder for them? These 4 men were trying to get to Jesus, because their friend needed Him, so that he would be healed. There were so many people in the way, they had to go through the roof, and lower him down to have Jesus heal him. What is in your way, when you are trying to find out more about Jesus? Is it what you watch, what you read, or all the other things you have going on? If it is important to you, you won't make excuses, you will do whatever it takes, whether it's for a friend, or for yourself. How far will you go to get closer to God, and do you believe you will be healed when you get there? One more little spin. Jesus saw the faith of the friends that brought him there, and healed the man because of "their" faith. Do you pray for other people?

Lord today I offer up prayers to You for all the people dealing with the loss of a loved, may You be with them in their time of sorrow.

Mark 2:1-12

January 17, 2015

Have you ever been around people and wondered if people thought less of you, because of the company you keep? Have you ever wondered if people had that feeling when they were with you? Who really are the righteous, and without sin? Jesus spent a lot of time with people who knew they were not righteous, and they followed Him, because they knew that. Why do some people feel they are not in need of this same grace? How hard is it to trust in God when it seems you have everything you need? When you are not feeling the pains of this world, it is easy to overlook God. Isn't that when we should be thankful to God for what we have? Do you feel you are among the righteous, or among the ones who need God's healing touch? Will you spend time with someone you know is not among the righteous?

Lord may I have the eyes to see those in most need of Your healing, and like You, never worry about what other people think about the company I keep.

Mark 2:13-17

January 18, 2015

What are you looking for? This is the question we should all ask ourselves. Jesus asks the two disciples this question, and they never really answer it. They ask Jesus where He is staying. Do you have an answer, or do you still have a lot of questions, also? What questions do you still want answers for, from God, in order to commit to following Him? Will you ever have all your answers? Do you take those questions to God in prayer, and do you truly listen for answers?

Lord, free my mind to hear You, and to know You more deeply.

John 1:35-42

January 19, 2015

Have you ever wondered why, as a Christian, other Christians will question the way you practice your faith, even to the point of questioning if you are a Christian? They did the same with Jesus, when the disciples of John the Baptist, and the Pharisees questioned why Jesus' disciples were not fasting. Just because people don't do the same things as you do, does not mean what they are doing is wrong. Because I am Catholic, and I am very open with my faith, I do get the same criticisms about what I believe as a Catholic. I started as a new wineskin, and have expanded with the knowledge that I was handed down, from the ones that taught me, and I have learned in my own studies. That doesn't make me wrong, it is just different than some other Christians may interpret. Do you have a hard time acknowledging other Christians, because of their understanding? Is there faith, in what they do? Does God appear to be present in their lives?

Lord may I be open minded enough, to trust that You work in each one of us, and not always the same.

Mark 2:18-22

January 20, 2015

How patient are you? Do you need quick answers to your prayers, or can you wait it out, because you trust God? Abraham is considered the father of both the Jewish, and Muslim faiths, because he trusted God's promise, even when tested, and having to wait for a son, until he was very old. He had two children, one from his made servant, that He named Ishmael, and one from his wife Sarah, who He named Isaac. Ishmael was the beginning of the Muslim nation, and Isaac was the beginning of the Jewish. Abraham trusted that God would fulfill His promise, and waited on God's promise for the son, that was to come. Do you have the patience to wait, and the faith to trust that God's promise will be fulfilled?

Lord, patience has always been my downfall, may You grant me the peace that comes with waiting for You!

Hebrews 6:10-20

January 21, 2015

Do you ever do things, just because it is the right thing to do, even when others don't approve of what you are doing? How bold are you, when you know you could be condemned for doing something that is right? Jesus could feel the Pharisees cold hands around His neck for what He was about to do, but doing what was right, He healed the man. Do you sometimes feel persecuted, and feel that you wouldn't do it any other way? This is a part of people that makes them struggle with their faith. This is when some people will justify their lack of faith, because it can cause persecution. Some will do what is right, every time, and some will compromise, for their own good. Do you stand up in the face of adversity, or will you walk away, to live another day? Where is your trust, in God, or in what people think of you, or your job? Will you withstand your daily tests?

Lord God, may Your Holy Spirit be with me as I go through the trials of the day. May I always know You are with me, and trust in You.

Mark 3:1-6

January 22, 2015

Do you sometimes feel the weight of the world crashing in on you? Sometimes it can be from the good that you do, and sometimes because of where you are at, and how you deal with pressure. Jesus felt the pressure of everyone wanting to be near him, and wanting to touch Him. He made sure He was able to get His message to the people, without being crushed, by having a boat ready that He could speak to the people in. Sometimes we need to see what is around us, and know that we are doing what is right, so we can continue doing what we are doing. We get comfortable in our surroundings, and we cannot see what can make the situation easier. Do you know your surroundings well enough to be ready for whatever comes your way? Do you trust that you are not in this thing all alone, and that God is always there to help provide that boat?

Lord, You have shown me the way, and sometimes I do not look to You first, may I always know You are willing to show me, if I would only look to You first.

Mark 3:7-12

January 23, 2015

How do you think Jesus would have treated Judas Iscariot? Would it have been revealed to Him from the beginning that Judas was the one to betray Him? I know I've asked this question before, but in our human minds it seems hard to understand how you would treat the person that you know is going to hand you over to be put to death. We think of death as the end, and Jesus saw it as the start of the Greatness that He was going to open for all of those who trust in Him. Death is the beginning of the life that we all try to aspire to here on earth, a life with no pain, no worries, no suffering, and no politics. However, we can't just enter on our own, we need to understand why we so desire Heaven, and live for the reward that is in Heaven. Part of our purpose is to help people understand why they would want to be in Heaven. Jesus chooses us for the specific task, that He knows we are capable of, even before we know we can do what He asks. Would you follow Jesus up that mountain, and follow Him, and do what He asks of you?

Lord, may I always see as You see, and follow You, knowing that You have the gift of everlasting life.

Mark 3:13-19

January 24, 2015

Are you so adamant about your faith that some people, and family members, think you're crazy? I remember people from high school that we used to call "holy rollers". Little did I know, I would be classified that way by some, when I finally found out who God is. There was a certain belittling to that name, but I really didn't know God at that time, and they obviously did. My question is, if you were one of them then, are you still, and if you're not, why aren't you? If you are going to be a "Fool" for something, wouldn't you want it to be for God? This reading is short, and yet very powerful. Jesus was not accepted by all of His family members because they thought He was a "wack job", talking all the time about God as His Father. Why is that so hard for some people? Yes it requires faith, but we all put our faith in something? What do people think of you, and do you care, if their impression of you is because of what God has done in your life? Will you speak out for God? Does God give you purpose?

Lord so many times You point out the things in my life, of who I was, and who I am now, may I continue to grow in Your most Holy love.

Mark 3:20-21

January 25, 2015

Have you ever had to hire people, or recruit volunteers for an organization or church function? When you do this, aren't you looking for the right character to make your group better, bigger, and stronger? It's not always the ones that are the most educated that can help you grow, it's the one that will learn, and buy into what your selling. The ones that will see the vision the way you see it, and want the same thing you want, are the best fit for you. Wouldn't Jesus have been looking for the same? He knew He had to teach them, but He also needed the type of person that would buy in 100%. Are you willing to follow Jesus, and buy in 100%? What do you need to do to be selected to be on Jesus' team? Do you have what it takes? Jesus selected ordinary people, do you fit that description?

Lord, You have asked me to commit to You, and I accept what you have offered, and the benefits that you offer. Thank you!

Mark 1:14-20

January 26, 2015

Do you believe in God? If you don't wouldn't that be exactly what Satan would want? Life is not like a sporting event, where you can decide that, I don't like either team, so I don't care who wins. Just because you deny that God or Satan exist, doesn't mean that they don't exist. The one thing I know is, there is a God, and if there is a God, there is evil, or Satan. The scribes were trying to convince people that Jesus was driving out demons by the power of Satan. If that was true, than we could sit back and watch Satan destroy himself? If you watch the news, you know that isn't happening. We can choose to have God in our corner, and have him be our armor, or we can say we don't believe in God, and be ruled by the evil that is Satan. Do you choose God over evil, or do you make the unconscious choice of being on Satan's side? Wouldn't Satan want you to deny he exists?

Lord, in You I find the peace that brings me through even the roughest days, may I always wear the armor that is You, to protect me.

Mark 3:22-30

January 27, 2015

Was Jesus disrespecting His mother and family when He said, "Who are my mother and my brothers?"? Why would He say that? He always honors His mother and family, because it is one of the Ten Commandments, to honor your mother and your father. This reading has nothing to do with denying His family, but everything to do with how He treats everyone who follows His word, and believes in Him. Do you trust in Jesus enough to be considered a family member? Would you be sitting around Him and listening to what He has to say, if there is something else to do? Do you make excuses not to spend more time with Him in prayer, and going to church? There is always something going on, but what do you consider more important?

Lord, may I always be available for You, and answer Your call when You need me to help carry out Your message. May I always share in Your family bond.

Mark 3:31-35

January 28, 2015

Have you grown in your faith, or was it just a passing fancy, and you don't have time for it anymore, or you just thought it was a lot of work? Some of you have been reading these post since I started, and some have just started reading them. This parable is for you no matter where you are in your faith journey. The people with gardens, and farmers will understand this parable right away, but some will need Jesus to explain it, and He does in this reading, so please take the time to read it. Have you grown roots, and become strong, or is there a lot of work to be done in you yet?

Lord may You continue to feed me with Your amazing teachings, that I may be there to help when called upon.

Mark 4:1-20

January 29, 2015

When you turn on a light, are you the only one who benefits from its radiance? If you use a lamp, it allows you to see, but doesn't it also brighten the way for others to see? If you're the only one benefiting from the light, wouldn't that be a flashlight? Why would you not want to help others see, especially if you have the light? If you are Christian and you do not share that light, aren't you then putting your light under a basket? There's a saying that says, "If you were being accused of being a Christian, would there be enough evidence to convict you?" Think about that for a minute or two. How do people see you, especially those that see you every day? Why wouldn't you want to share the light with everyone in the room? When we do not fear other people's opinions of us, we tend to be free to share our light. Will you make it known that you have a light that brightens your day, and in turn, brightens the day for those around you?

Lord may Your light shine on me, and may I in turn radiate that same light out for others to see and use.

Mark 4:21-25

January 30, 2015

Have you ever wondered how wild plants continue on with no one replanting them? The birds eat the seeds and while flying, they excrete them out in new areas, and the seeds, being already fertilized, grow on their own with a little water and sun. Why would Jesus use a parable about a mustard seed, and birds in the branches of the tree once it has grown? We are the mustard seed. Sometimes we are chewed up, and sent out to fend for ourselves, but given the right circumstances we grow, and are able to supply food and hope for others. I think we've all experienced part of this message, but have you grown afterword, or are you still lying in the mess that was created, waiting for someone else to put you where they think you need to be? Do you trust that God will provide you with all you need?

Lord may Your Son, and the food and water that is Your word, continue to strengthen me, that I may grow and flourish, as You have planned for me.

Mark 4:26-304

January 31, 2015

When the times are tough and it seems like the waves are crashing down on you, do you call out to God who is always with you? Do you realize He is always with you? Do you know that He can calm the roughest waters, and storms in your life? Jesus didn't wake up from the storm, until the disciples woke Him, because He never feared anything of this world. Do you fear the things of this world? So many times we have death, and near death, staring us in the face, and we tremble because of doubt of what is to come. If you are secure in knowing there is something greater than what is in this world, why should we have fear? The trials we face in this world are just that, trials. How do you face the reality of this world? Do you trust that God will bring you through it, and if He doesn't, isn't what's to come a better place?

Lord may I know You are with me always, and when the fear and anxiety of uncertainty look me in the face, my I always know You can comfort me, and bring to where You are.

Mark 4:35-41

February 1, 2015

Are you married and/or have children? How much free time do you have? If you are married, don't you usually want to spend your free time with your spouse? If you have children, don't you usually want time with them? When my children were younger, it seems I couldn't spend enough time with them, and now when they come home, I want to spend most of my time with them. How hard is it to fit everything, and God into your life, especially if your job, or life commitment, was to serve God? In today's reading from Paul to the Corinthians, we see why the Catholic Church and a few other religions have chosen to not have married priests, or pastors. It is a little hard to devote your time fully to God, when you have to wrestle with time, and priorities. Do you make time for God a priority, or is it just something you fit in if you are in need of Him? Is it too hard to make time for God even on Sunday?

Lord, You have given me purpose, and understanding, may I always give You my time as You deserve.

1 Corinthians 7:32-35

February 2, 2015

How hard is it for you to take advice from someone who can't relate to who you are, or where you have come from? Isn't it somewhat reassuring knowing that you have a lot in common with someone, when they are trying to console you? You tend to be a little more receptive to people that share your experiences. Jesus could have come as a king and ruled over the world, the way the scribes and Pharisees expected Him to come, but He didn't. He came as a common person, with a common life, to show us He understands where we come from. He shared in our fears, He shared in the trials of what this life offers, and He even experienced the type of death that we hope to never experience. He came as one of us, so we would understand that He can relate to whatever we are going through. Does He give you reason for hope? Do you trust that Jesus knows you enough to give you the strength needed to overcome whatever this world throws at you?

Lord through Your grace, I see, and through Your example, I live. May that be enough for me to live as You have shown me.

Hebrews 2:14-18

February 3, 2015

How proud are you? Are you so proud that you would risk your life, or a family members, to not let other people know you have faith in God? Jairus was a synagogue official that risked his job, and livelihood to show his faith, and heal his daughter. It seems we would all do that if a life was dependent on it, but what would it take for you? Are you someone that people know to have an open faith? How far would you go to reach out and touch Jesus, in a large crowd of people? Will you do whatever it takes to be healed, even if your friends and family don't understand?

Lord, You have given me the strength and courage to reach out to You, may I always trust in Your healing power.

Mark 5:21-43

February 4, 2015

How many of you were disciplined as a child? Most likely, all of you. How many are so afraid of upsetting your children, that you have found mild ways of disciplining them, so they don't cry? First off, I'm not advocating beating your children. So many times we think that we need to make their life easier, because we had it so tough when we grew up. Our parents may have beat our butts when we did something wrong, but we usually learned not to do that again. Most times we don't understand the struggles that God is putting us through, and that may be one reason some people say, "If there is a God, He wouldn't allow suffering in the world". How many have learned more from your pains, than from your joy? We have memories of our joy, but we learn from our pains. Why do you suppose I ask so many questions in these posts? I very seldom answer them, because if you want to know the answer, you will ask God, or search the answers out, because we learn from what we have to struggle through. Do you experience pain and suffering? Have you become stronger because of it?

Lord, I have become a stronger person because of the disciplines You have allowed me to experience, may I remember that You are always my God, and have experienced more suffering on the cross than I could bare.

Hebrews 12:4-7, 11-15

February 5, 2015

How much do you trust that God will provide for you? How many times have you been sent on a task, and you felt God was directing you, but you weren't really sure what was going to happen? Jesus sent out the apostles, two by two, and told them to teach repentance. They were not to take anything extra, they were to trust that God would provide for them. In the process, they healed people, because when we repent of our sins, we can be healed physically as well as spiritually. Do you know the healing power that asking forgiveness can bring to you? Have you really thought about what may be considered a sin in God's eyes? Will you trust Him with your life, if it is asked of you to go without your possessions?

Lord please forgive me for not always thinking of where I came from, and where You have brought me to, may I be forgiven of those sins deep in my heart.

Mark 6:7-13

February 6, 2015

When is the last time you were aware that you were entertaining angels? The writer of this letter to the Hebrews mentions that we sometimes entertain them when we are unaware of it. Many years ago, while driving home, I noticed a car stuck in the drain ditch next to their driveway. I pulled over to see if I could help. With three adults in the car, none were able to help due to their health. I thought they were going to need a tractor to pull them out, but I thought I would give it a try. I was able to push them out, apparently, with a little help, because one of the ladies asked if I was an Angel. I wasn't really sure why she asked me that, but maybe because there was no physical way I should have been able to push that car out of the ditch with three adults in the car. Sometimes we need help, and don't ask for it, but the angels are still there. Are you aware of the angels in your life? Do you keep God always near you?

Lord, open my eyes to see You, and to always be aware of Your presence, and may Your Angels be always with me through this life.

Hebrews 13:1-8

February 7, 2015

Do you take time to step away and reflect on the things that have happened? The last time we heard from the Apostles, Jesus was sending them away two by two, to teach repentance. Now they are returning with their own stories of what they saw, and accomplished. Jesus takes them away to rest, and teach them more about what has happened. We need that time to share with God in prayer, the things that have changed our lives, and to understand, sometimes what has really happened. Do you spend time in quiet prayer, away from all the hustle and bustle, in total silence, and listen to what God has to say about your day? Try getting in a comfortable place, and sit in total silence, where you won't be disrupted, open with saying hi to God, and listen to what He has to say.

Lord, open my mind, that I may truly listen to You, and trust that You are there speaking to me.

Mark 6:30-34

February 8, 2015

Do you ever read the Bible, and see something that hits you right in the face, like you wrote it, or live it? This letter from Paul to the Corinthians is just that reading for me. I have been doing these reflections for at least two years, around the same time every day. Sometimes I don't feel like doing it, and I'm sure there are some people that wish I would stop, but there are some that read them nearly every day, so I continue. So many times we feel that way with our jobs, but do you go to work for you, or is there something bigger that you should be accomplishing? Is your work life there for you to accomplish something for God, or are you just there waiting for payday? We can work for a greater purpose than just a check. Think about that the next time you head to work. Who are you really working for?

Lord, the people of this world are all Yours, may I remember that, in my job, and all that I do. To You be the Glory!

1 Corinthians 9:16-19, 22-23

February 9, 2015

Do you search out God, or do you just hope to come across Him along your daily path? When you find Him, are you looking for Him to perform some miracle, or are you looking for Him, because you need Him in your daily life? Many times, people will seek and find Jesus, to help them out in a tough situation, or for healing, and after they have gotten through that tough time, they move on with their life and forget about what He has done for them. We are like that saying that says, "What have you done for me lately?" If you seek God to be part of your life, He is like that best friend, who will be there in the good times and the bad times, because He wants to share in both. Even when you don't think you need Him, He is there. Have you been seeking God? Have you found the friend that is always beside you?

Lord, thank You for being with me when I wasn't aware of Your presence, but like a good friend, You had my back.

Mark 6:53-56

February 10, 2015

Do you honor your mother and your father? Some of us are reaching an age when the parents start to need the same help as a child would. Parents are getting older, and the ones that cared for you, and nourished you as a child, now need you to provide that same love to them. Do you take your time, and your money to provide that same love to them? Some of us have lost their parents, and wish we were able to see them one more time, even if it required waiting on them, and providing for them. We don't always realize what we have until it's gone. Anytime a loved one is lost, we miss them, and desire one more day with them. Do you care for your parents, like it's the last day you will be with them?

Lord, I thank you for my parents, and ask that you tell them I love them, and miss them.

Mark 7:1-13

February 11, 2015

Do you ever think about what you watch, read, eat, drink, and listen to? Have you ever thought how that helps to make you who you are? When Jesus says that, "nothing that enters the body can defile that person, but what comes from within is what will defile" (Mark 7:15), even the disciples were not understanding it. Jesus was criticizing some of the Jewish laws that told them what they could and could not eat. With all of our modern technology, I'm sure Jesus might elaborate on that a little more. Do the things that you read, watch, and listen to affect what you say and do? Do they make you a better person, or someone that needs to be tolerated, or avoided? Words and actions can hurt people, but are you hurting the soul of the people you are around? We do have some choice as to what we are exposed to, but are you exposing the weak to things they are not able to deal with? What can you do to make your actions, and words not destroy or damage a soul?

Lord, You know this is probably my biggest weakness, may I always remember that the soul I may damage still has your Holy Spirit also.

Mark 7:14-23

February 12, 2015

Have you ever wondered if you are a chosen one of God? Does God play favorites? Jesus goes to a town that is not part of the Jewish community, in fact it is full of people that probably have very little faith in any sort of God. The woman in the story is apparently disparate to make her daughter well again, and has heard about this man who is healing people. Did Jesus come to this town to show them who God is, and let them know that nobody is far removed from God? Did He want the people to see what faith really is? This woman was not going to go away until something was done to help her daughter. She asked Jesus why she was not good enough, and He told her that her faith, has healed her daughter. She didn't say, "How do I know she is healed?" she trusted that her daughter was healed. Is your faith strong enough to challenge God, when you really don't understand? Do you continue to go to Him, even when He says no?

Lord, thank You for always being there, even when I struggle, and don't notice Your presence. May I always have the faith and persistence to come to You.

Mark 7:24-30

February 13, 2015

Is there more to the healings that we read in the Bible, than we actually see? Jesus heals the deaf person, who also has a speech impediment, and he can now hear, and speak clearly. I have friends and relatives who have hearing disabilities, and they also have speech impediments. When you don't hear clearly, it always seems to affect your speech, and confidence in your speech. Are you able to speak clearly and confidentially about God, and the life of Jesus? Are you hearing God clearly enough to be confident in speaking about Him? Do you attend church, and hear the message that God wants you to hear? If you hear it, do you share it with the people you love, and even the people you don't care much about? Why hear, and see, if you won't speak and share? How can God open your eyes and ears, so that you can speak about Him?

Lord You have removed my fear, and opened my eyes, and ears, may I freely speak about You every chance I get.

Mark 7:31-37

February 14, 2015

Have you ever been so consumed with what is going on around you that you didn't even think about eating? My family will tell you that doesn't really happen to me very often. I tend to get a little hard to be around when I am hungry. The crowd was following Jesus, and He fed them for three days, with just His word. They weren't complaining, they were eating everything Jesus had to say, and that was satisfying them. Jesus was moved with pity for them, and so He also gave them the food they needed for nourishment. When you follow Jesus, He feeds your soul, and He provides the nourishment for our bodies. The people weren't asking for food, their soul was being fed, so they were not feeling the desire for anything else. Have you been so consumed with God's word, that He removed all your other earthly desires? Has God fed your soul?

My God, and my Lord, You provide the everlasting word, that sustains my soul.

Mark 8:1-10

February 15, 2015

Do you treat people differently when you know some dirt about them? Do you avoid them if you know they have a disease? Do you let people know you have a disease or illness? This reading from Leviticus is one of the Old laws handed down from Moses. If you had to let people know your sins every time you saw them, would you? Most people noticed the signs of leprosy, and would probably stay away anyhow, but they don't see our sins, so they come to us unknowing. Some people have sins that could hurt a person more than even leprosy. Wouldn't it be worse to damage someone's soul, than to damage their physical appearance? How much harder is it to heal spiritually, than to heal physically? Are you aware of your sins? Have you acknowledged them to God, and let Him know You are aware of your sins?

Lord may I always come to you to acknowledge my sins, for my own healing. Thank you Lord for the sacrament of reconciliation. Thank you Father Tom for the insight on this reading.

Leviticus 13:1-2, 44-46

February 16, 2015

Do you ever share your faith with other people, and they still don't understand your faith in God, and they want some sort of proof or a sign? Even Jesus, while walking this earth, was questioned about proof, and the Pharisees wanted a sign from God. Jesus argued with them, and all the while, God was right in front of them, and they could not see the sign. Jesus finally said there will not be a sign given to them, because they were blind to seeing a sign. There are quite a few people that read these posts regularly that ask me for signs. I try to show them, but only by faith will they see, and I cannot change their faith, they have to do it. I am comforted by knowing that even people who saw Jesus, would still ask for a sign. Does your faith allow you to see the signs from God? Do you get discouraged when people will still not believe? Jesus didn't stop performing miracles because some people didn't believe did He?

Lord may Your love continue to grow in me, and the people who see You, that we may be the sign they so wish to see.

Mark 8:11-13

February 17, 2015

When you do see a miracle do you know what it means? Many of us have seen, or been a part of a miracle, but what is the purpose of that miracle? Is it just to let you know God exists? The disciples had seen many of Jesus' miracles, including the multiplication of the loaves, and fish, and just thought they were ways to prove that Jesus is God? They didn't really think about the deeper meaning. Jesus helps them to understand by making them think about what had happened. Why would He feed so many, with so little? Could it be to let them know, as long as you keep God close to you, God will provide what you need? The disciples worried about having enough to eat, and forgot all about the bread and fish miracles. When you're stressed and troubled, do you forget that God is always there, and will provide what you need?

Lord may I always be aware that everything I have is because of You, and know that it has never been mine to begin with, but a gift from You.

Mark 8:14-21

February 18, 2015

Do you acknowledge your sins? Today is Ash Wednesday, and for many Christians the start of Lent. Lent is 40 days of fasting, not counting Sundays, before Easter. The fast is a time of acknowledging your sins, and your faithfulness to God, and giving up of something that you have grown fond of, to realize that it is given to you by God. It can also be a time of doing for others, and making your life more complete by the giving of your surplus, or time and gifts. Take some time to reflect on what you have, and what you have done, and what you could do, or do differently. Is there something that you feel is not good for you, or that you enjoy too much, that you can do without for 40 days, to see how God can provide, in that time of desire? When you do without, you reflect on why you are giving up, and ask God to help you understand, "why?" This Psalm is a great reflection, and acknowledgement of our sinfulness.

Lord be with me during this Lenten season, help me to see You, and know that you will never abandon me, even in my lowest moments. Grant me the strength to resist when I am weak.

Psalms 51:3-6ab, 12-14 and 17

February 19, 2015

How hard would it be to be following someone, and see all those miracles performed, then have Him tell you, He will be put to death? If that wasn't bad enough, then He tells you, if you want to follow Him, you will have to pick up your cross, Daily? He told them it would not be easy to be a follower. If you are a believer, there is not a lot of commitment in that, but if you are a follower of Christ, you will have to "pick up your cross Daily". When you follow, you are also with Christ, and He will help you carry that cross, but you need to be committed. This time of Lent, you will be challenged with why you are giving up something, or doing something extra, in the name of fasting. It will not always be easy, but remember why you made that commitment, it is to bring you closer to God. Are you giving up something that you know you will struggle with? Are you planning on doing something that will not always be easy?

Lord may I be a committed follower, and know that when I struggle, You will always be with me.

Luke 9:22-25

February 20, 2015

Is your fast a time of despair, or is a time of doing for others? There is a good lesson to be learned from the prophet Isaiah. You will feel blessed by helping others, and giving of yourself, during these days of Lent. You may even find yourself doing it more when Lent is over. How will God change you, to allow you to make changes in the lives of others?

The prayer of St. Francis: Lord, make me an instrument of your peace, Where there is hatred, let me sow love; where there is injury, pardon; where there is doubt, faith; where there is despair, hope; where there is darkness, light; where there is sadness, joy; O Divine Master, grant that I may not so much seek to be consoled as to console; to be understood as to understand; to be loved as to love. For it is in giving that we receive; it is in pardoning that we are pardoned; and it is in dying that we are born to eternal life.

Isaiah 58:1-9a

February 21, 2015

What does it mean to follow someone? When you follow, that means you are with them, and they will lead the way. If they show you the way and you stay on that path, doesn't that mean they will clear the path, or remove the troubles before you? What happens when you stray from the path? You have to clear that path, right? Sometimes we don't like the easy path, because we want the challenge that comes from making your own path, and not following. We want to be the leader. The problem with that in the realm of the spiritual, is we don't have the strength to overcome the trees in our way, without help. Jesus tells Levi (he becomes Matthew) to "follow me". (Luke 5:27) He shows Levi the way, and leads him, and helps him to remove the obstacles before Him. Will you follow Jesus' lead and search out the people who are begging for direction? Will you show someone that Jesus is the leader, who won't let you down?

Lord may I follow You always, and know that You are there for me when I feel the frustration, and need help seeing the way to our Heavenly Father.

Luke 5:27-32

February 22, 2015

If you have given up something for Lent, how have you been doing so far? It seems like the first week is somewhat easy, but after the first week, it seems harder. Lent is a great way to challenge yourself and test your resolve, to doing what you commit to. Jesus was in the desert for 40 days and challenged by Satan, and lived among the wild beasts, but the Angels were also there to minister to Him. You will be tested, but you are not alone in this. One more note, for those who went to Ash Wednesday services. When you receive the ashes, they make the sign of the cross, and repeat from this scripture. "Repent, and believe in the gospel" (Mark 1: 15). Will you be strong when the challenge, or temptation is before you?

Lord, with You I am strong, may I know You are with me always, and that You are with me, when I am weak.

Mark 1:12-15

February 23, 2015

What makes you give, or not give, help, or not help, when someone is in need? Do you first have to determine if the ones in need, are truly in need, or trying to take advantage of you? Have we been so used by people, that we have stopped helping the ones that are truly in need? What do you consider using the system? Do we hear about so many scams that we have to do our own research before we give to some new charity? What makes you give your time or money, and what makes you not give? Do you love yourself more than you love others?

Lord, open my heart, and open my eyes to see You, in those in need.

Matthew 25:31-46

February 24, 2015

When is the last time you prayed "The Our Father", or The Lord's Prayer"? Have you ever prayed it very slowly, and focused on the words? Jesus taught us this prayer, not to be our only prayer, but to show us how to pray. At the end of this scripture you will see one of the things He wants us to focus on. How do you forgive those who have sinned against you? Do you forgive them, or is that something you have a very hard time with? What if God forgave you, or didn't forgive you, the way you forgive? Jesus tells us that if we can't forgive, how can we expect God to forgive. I challenge you to repeat the prayer Jesus taught us, every morning, and every night, until Easter. See if it changes your outlook on others, and yourself. Will you take that challenge?

Lord, forgive me of my sins, as I forgive those who have sinned against me.

Matthew 6:7-15

February 25, 2015

Have you ever thought about what made you become Christian, or for the people raised in a Christian family, a firmer believer in Christ? Was it acknowledging you were a sinner, and knowing you were capable of more? Some people don't think they sin, or think they are "not too bad", so they don't repent. In the Gospel of Luke, Jesus tells us, "At the judgment, the men of Nineveh will arise with this generation and condemn it, because at the preaching of Jonah they repented, and there is something greater than Jonah here." (Luke 11:32) The reading from the book of Jonah, is what Jesus was referencing. All the people repented of their sins, and the king told everyone to do the same. If someone told you the end was near, would you change, or would you think it was just some kook trying to make a difference?

I confess to almighty God and to you, my brothers and sisters, that I have greatly sinned, in my thoughts and in my words, in what I have done and in what I have failed to do, through my fault, through my fault, through my most grievous fault; therefore I ask blessed Mary ever-Virgin, all the Angels and Saints, and you, my brothers and sisters, to pray for me to the Lord our God. Amen.

Jonah 3:1-10

February 26, 2015

Do you remember, as a child, asking your parents for something? It was always hit or miss, whether you would actually get what you asked for. Maybe that's why as adults, we are unsure if we will get what we ask for from God. Even as children, we learned that persistence does pay off, yet we don't always do that when it comes to asking for something from God. When you remember God as The Father, you realize that He loves you, and wants what is best for you, or will make you happy, because no "good father" wants to see his child upset. Do you go to God with the full confidence that He will heal your friend, or loved one? Do you go in confidence to ask for the things you need?

Lord, for the many people on my friends and family list, that are struggling with health, and dealing with loss, may You heal their broken hearts, and provide the healing they desire.

Matthew 7:7-12

February 27, 2015

Have you ever wondered if God will ever accept you, and forgive you, for what you have done? Jesus has washed away our sins, and He has reconciled us by His dying on the cross, but sometimes we have a hard time believing that we can be forgiven for what we have done. Even before Jesus Christ died on the cross, the prophet Ezekiel talked about God's forgiveness. It is interesting however, that he also talks about how the virtuous man can turn from his ways, and be evil. Think about the people that have led people to God, and became evil, and did atrocious things. All the good that they did, will not save them from their final destination. Evil is there waiting for you to either extinguish it, or feed it. Will you allow it to continue to grow, or will you bring the soothing waters of Jesus' forgiveness in, to extinguish the evil?

O my Jesus, forgive us our sins, save us from the fires of Hell; lead all souls to Heaven, especially those in most need of Your mercy.

Ezekiel 18:21-28

(1 Peter 5:8 NAB) Be sober and vigilant. Your opponent the devil is prowling around like a roaring lion looking for [someone] to devour.

February 28, 2015

How hard is it for you to pray for someone that you don't agree with, or have even had disputes with? Didn't God create them as well as you? We all have differences in opinion, because none of us were raised in the same situation. We can't agree 100% with anyone, even our own siblings, or children. Yes we can agree on some things, but not everything. This Gospel is the heart and soul of what it means to be a Christian. Even though we can't always agree, we can still pray for those who persecute us. It is great therapy, because when you pray for someone you do disagree with, you start to feel a certain compassion for them. When is the last time you prayed for someone you had an argument with, or that did something to you, that you find hard to forgive?

Lord I pray that You help me to see my own fault, in what I do and say, that I may be forgiven as well as forgive.

Matthew 5:43-48

March 1, 2015

Have you ever heard God speaking to you? We don't always realize when He speaks to us, because we think we are too insignificant for Him to speak to us. Jesus took Peter, John, and James with Him to the mountain, probably knowing full well what was about to happen. They heard God say to them, "This is my beloved Son. Listen to Him"(Mark 9:7). The three of them remembered, and shared this story after Jesus' resurrection, but were too terrified when Jesus was crucified to remember. Too often we are in a situation that is so traumatic that we don't recall the places that God has taken us, and what He has said to us. Can you think of a time when you know God was with you, and you saw something, or heard something that you know could only be from God? Do you remember that when you are having a time in your life that you are struggling through?

Lord You are with me in my times of good, and in my times of need, may I always remember to call upon You, in good times and in bad.

Mark 9:2-10

March 2, 2015

What does it mean to be merciful? Jesus tells us to be merciful, as your Father is merciful. It means to have compassion, or to care about someone who is suffering, and want to help them, no matter what the cost. Do you have compassion when someone is in need? It seems like there is always someone in need. When someone is hurting and you can't be physically present, you can always pray for them. If you were in the same situation, isn't there a certain amount of comfort knowing someone is praying for you? They may not be able to make it, but their prayers may bring the person that can comfort us. Will you give more than is expected of you?

Lord may I be merciful, as You are merciful. May the compassion You have shown me, be the same compassion I share.

Luke 6:36-38

March 3, 2015

How do you treat your brothers and sisters? Do you treat them better, or worse than other people you know? Some people will tell you, they don't get along with their siblings, but that is usually the minority. Some may not get along with them, but as soon as someone attacks them, they are "all in". There is something about, blood relations that we don't understand. Jesus tells us that we are all brothers. Does that make you look at people differently? We have one Father, who is in Heaven. Why do we have so many disagreements with each other, much less our own brothers and sisters? There are Christian brothers and sisters, that have a preconceived, or learned understanding about what other Christian denominations believe, and have decided they all must be like that, so have decided not to get along. Who are your brothers and sisters? Would you stand with them to the bitter end?

Lord may I see all people the way You see people, and know that You made each one of us, that I will know they are my brothers and sisters.

Matthew 23:1-12

March 4, 2015

Have you ever thought real hard about your purpose here on earth? Have you ever really wondered, "What's it all about?" Some people tend to dwell on this a little too much, and make themselves depressed. Do you stay close to God, and ask Him to guide you through your day, and to help you see what you need to do? Jesus had a purpose while He was here, and He wanted to make sure the disciples understood, they too had a purpose. They are to serve others, and not be concerned about here, or what will become of us. Do you give it all to God, and trust Him with your life, and your destination?

Lord You ask me to serve, rather than be served, may I be Your servant, and do as You ask.

Matthew 20:17-28

March 5, 2015

What do you need to hear or see, to convince you to live a life for God? Jesus tells the parable of the rich man and Lazarus, and how some people will hear what they would need to change, and even see someone raised from the dead, and will not change. If there is not a Heaven, or a Hell, would it really matter? What if the only thing was Heaven, and there was no Hell? Would it really matter? Apparently, the rich man didn't think there was a Hell, and it didn't matter how he lived his life. Will you be enjoying a life with God, or will you be wishing you would have understood, when you had the chance? WITH GOD, without God, WITH HIM, or without Him?

Lord I pray today for those who have lived without knowing You, that You may send the person into their life, that can help them know You, and understand.

Luke 16:19-31

March 6, 2015

How well do you understand the parables of Jesus, when you read them? Even the disciples asked questions about what was meant. Jesus was speaking to the Pharisees and scribes when telling this parable. He was showing them how all of God's prophets were sent, and now God is sending His Son, and they will treat Him the same. They understood, but they also did not want to believe that Jesus is the Son of God. Even when we see the truth, and hear it, we sometimes will still not want to believe. Do you ask God to help you understand what you have read?

My Lord, and my God, may You guide me in what I read, and what I hear, that Your Holy Spirit will help me know You more deeply.

Matthew 21:33-43, 45-46

March 7, 2015

Where do you see yourself, when you think about forgiveness? This is the longest parable Jesus tells, but it has many lessons about forgiveness, and understanding. Are you the wayward, misguided son who just wants forgiveness, or are you the son who has always lived your life as God would want, but can't understand the forgiveness of your Father? Are you like the Father, and have learned how to forgive, out of love and loss? Think about who you most resemble, when reading, and meditating on this parable.

My God, and my Father, may I know how to forgive as You forgive.

Luke 15:1-3, 11-32

March 8, 2015

Do you think of your body as a temple of the Holy Spirit? It is you know! When you eat, drink, and go out, do you remember that it is a temple? Jesus comes to the temple and clears out the area of all that is wrong, and unholy. He does the same to our bodies, when we invite Him to be a part of our lives. Sometimes that is the hardest for us to let him clean, because we have grown accustomed to all of our old habits, and our own destructive ways. Will you let Jesus clear the junk out of your life, or will you fight it off, because you don't think what you are doing is that bad?

Jesus, You have the words, and power of everlasting life, clean out the old ways of my life, that Your Holy Spirit may reside in me.

John 2: 13-25

March 9, 2015

Why is it that people have less respect for, someone claiming to have a voice from God, when they know them from their own town, or their relatives? Is it because you know their history, or better yet, their family's history? We have a hard time believing that we know someone that can go from what we thought them to be, to being someone speaking of God. Even Jesus was not able to convince the people of Nazareth that He was speaking for God. He was chased out of the town, and had to flee for His life. Do you speak boldly enough about your faith, that you are sometimes shunned? If not, does that mean you're not speaking up enough?

Lord grant me the strength to speak boldly about You, and the wisdom to know when it's time to move on.

Luke 4:24-30

March 10, 2015

Have you ever asked for forgiveness, and received it, and not notice that you were unable to forgive someone? The first servant in this parable was forgiven his debt, and seemed very grateful for that forgiveness, but was unable to provide the same kind of forgiveness to his fellow man. Sometimes we are wronged in such a way, that it has an impact on us personally, and possibly, physically, and it cut some deep wounds. It seems impossible to forgive someone, when there are scars. Think about how you may have offended someone, or even God, and desperately need that forgiveness to help your wounds, and even your scars, to heal. Do you need to forgive someone that it seems impossible to forgive? Do you need the healing that forgiving someone else, can provide?

Lord, may I have the opportunity to forgive those who I have not been able to forgive, and ask forgiveness of those I have offended.

Matthew 18:21-35

March 11, 2015

Do you do whatever it takes to make sure the children, and impressionable people, around you are not negatively affected by your actions, or words? The laws that God put forward in the first few books of the Bible are as relevant today as they were when they were first written. As a culture, we have changed laws to fit the pressures of people that don't think they are fair, but just because human law says something is not against the law, that doesn't change God's law. Jesus says He did not come to abolish the law, but to fulfill it. I know there are laws when we read them now, that don't seem to make sense to us in this day and age, but in their time, it was very much understood. Do you obey, and teach the commandments, or do you break them, and teach them to others?

Lord, to whom shall we go? You have the words of everlasting life. (John 6:68)

Matthew 5:17-19

March 12, 2015

Is it possible to ride the fence, on matters of spirituality? If you say I don't believe in Heaven or in Hell, does that mean you have nothing to worry about? Isn't the Holy Spirit the protector of our soul? If you don't acknowledge Him, will He still protect you? Most people will admit that there is good and evil in the world, but will not always admit that there is a spiritual force involved. Jesus tells the critics, "Whoever is not with me is against me, and whoever does not gather with me scatters."(Luke 11:23) Doesn't that mean you have to choose a side? Wouldn't you want the stronger man protecting your soul? If you can't ride the fence, which side would you pick?

Lord, may I always acknowledge that You are with me always and everywhere, and you will protect me in my times of struggle against evil.

Luke 11:14-23

March 13, 2015

Who is your neighbor? Isn't that anyone you may come across, on any given day? When you see someone, anyone, while walking or passing them in the store, on the street, or at work, do you acknowledge them by at least saying, "Hi!"? What if you're having a bad day, and someone says hi to you, completely out of the blue, and unexpected? Doesn't that make you feel better? That's what it means to love your neighbor as yourself. If it would make you feel better, wouldn't it also make someone else feel better? What would happen if today you said hi to everyone you meet, or hold the door for the next person? What if you went out of your way to help someone? Would it make a difference?

Jesus, You have taught me so many simple lessons, may I put those lessons into practice, in my daily life.

Mark 12:28-34

March 14, 2015

Have you ever really thought about your prayer life? Do you pray to God, or do you pray to yourself? Jesus compares the prayers of a tax collector and a Pharisee. They are both praying, but only one is humble and acknowledging that he is a sinful man, and needs God's help to become a better person. The other assumes he is everything that God wants him to be. Do you acknowledge that you need God, and that He can make you a better person, or do you think you have this under control, and don't need God in your life? Isn't it hard to listen to someone who is boasting about themselves? Isn't it easier to listen to someone that is asking for your help, and knows you will listen? Do you acknowledge who you really are?

Lord forgive me of my sinfulness, may I know I always need You to guide me.

Luke 18:9-14

March 15, 2015

What do you do for your children to give them hope, and life, that some people just would never understand? Do you love them so much, that you would step in for them with your life, no matter what they have done, or may do? Jesus points out the serpent that Moses lifted up in the desert to save the Israelites. They were being bitten by poisonous snakes because of the evil they did, but God gave them this serpent on a stick, so that if they touched it, they would live. This was to point to Jesus being hung on a cross, and dying for our sins, no matter what we have done, or may do. That's why today, you still see crucifixes in Catholic Churches, and homes, to remind us what God did for us. Do you move toward the light, or do you prefer to be in the darkness? For God so loved the world that He gave His only Son, so that everyone who believes in Him might not perish, but have eternal life. (John 3:16) Do you know that kind of love for your children, or for anyone else?

Lord may I know that kind of love, and know that You have always loved us more.

John 3:14-21

March 16, 2015

How hard is it for you to seek help, when you know the people that you socialize with will not understand what you are doing, and maybe even mock you because of it? How about if the help you need is for a family member? The royal official in this reading was desperate to get help for his son, and went to the one person who had been performing miracles, and healing people everywhere, even though it was against everything he stood for. He was not a supporter of Judaism, and Jesus was the largest religious figure of His day, yet he went to Him because he was desperate. Why is it that we only come to God when we are desperate? Are we that afraid, that people will think we are weak? The royal official knew what he did was right, because he never questioned Jesus, and then his whole family came to believe in Jesus' healing power. Are you desperate, and need the healing of Jesus in your life? How about a friend or family member that needs your prayer for their healing?

Lord today I offer up to You all of my friends and family that are desperate for your healing, that you may show them Your healing power.

John 4:43-54

March 17, 2015

Are you someone who longs for healing? Do you think healing will never come to you? The partially paralyzed man lay next to the pool that was thought to heal people for 38 years before Jesus came to him. The first thing Jesus asks him is, "Do you want to be well?"(John5:6) This is interesting because sometimes we want people to know our illness, sometimes for sympathy, but the illness has become such a part of our life that we may not want the healing. The illness becomes part of our identity. If you are healed, will you be like Peter's mother-in-law, who was healed and immediately got up and started serving Jesus and everyone around? Do you want to be healed to serve? If you pray for healing, is it for your own good, or for the good of God?

Father, Son, and Holy Spirit, may Your healing hand heal me and guide my way. May I be a servant of Your love.

John 5:1-16

March 18, 2015

If someone told you that they don't think Jesus is the Son of God, but only a prophet, or a wise man, or even a good man, how would you respond? Would a prophet, or a good man, or a wise man lie to the point of death? Why would Jesus say He is the Son of God, if He was a prophet, or a wise man, or a good man? Wouldn't He be lying if He isn't the Son of God? Jesus is questioned here about His claim, but He doesn't try to back away from His claim, He elaborates on it. What would you tell someone if they claimed that Jesus is not the Son of God? If they don't believe this, than they are saying Jesus is lying. Are you good with that?

Lord, even though You not need me to come to Your defense, I will stand for what You have taught me.

John 5:17-30

March 19, 2015

What does it mean to have a faith that people will not understand, and that could alter your standing, in the community? Do you care what people think of you? Most people will say they don't care what anybody thinks of them, yet they do things that say differently. Today the Catholic Church honors Joseph, the surrogate father of Jesus, for his faithfulness in trusting God, and having faith enough to be the protector of Jesus and Mary. He trusted that what he heard from God, to take Mary, even though she was already with child, and know that she is carrying God's only son, who was conceived of the Holy Spirit. Do you trust in God enough to put, whatever people may think of you, on the line, and risk whatever you think is yours?

Lord, thank you for the people that You have given us, to help us see what true faith in You is.

Matthew 1:16, 18-21, 24a

March 20, 2015

Do you ever have trouble trying to figure out what the scriptures are actually saying to you? If you do, you are like the majority of people. Even the people that studied the scriptures, back in Jesus' time read the scriptures, and thought they knew what was meant, but still did not understand. In this reading, you see Jesus point out that, even though they knew what was said, they didn't understand it. If you read Wisdom 2:12-22, you see a prophecy about when Jesus comes, and people knowing He is the Holy one of God, but they can't handle the truth, and opt to test Jesus, and persecute Him, to see if God will save Him. Do you pray that the Holy Spirit will guide you as you read scripture, to help you understand?

Holy Spirit, grant me understanding of Your Holy Word, and guide me, to know You more deeply.

John 7:1-2, 10, 25-30

March 21, 2015

Do you see the scriptures differently than you did when you first started reading these reflections? Sometimes our eyes are opened to seeing as God wants us to see, and we realize that we weren't looking at things the way we do now. The guards were sent to arrest Jesus, and after hearing Him speak, they realized there was something special in Him, and they wanted to listen to Him. Because they heard, and were convinced that He was more than the Pharisees made Him out to be, they listened with their heart, and didn't arrest Him. Do you listen to what God says to you, and trust Him, or do you listen to what the world is telling you, and trust them more? Who's hands do you put your eternal life into?

Lord I trust in You, and know that only You provide me with everlasting life.

John 7:40-53

March 22, 2015

Have you had to endure suffering and pain, or even watch someone else go through it, and wondered why? Why shouldn't we endure suffering? Who ever said we wouldn't? In Jesus' last days, even He had to endure the same pain and suffering, and asked His Father if He should have to go through with it. Don't we also learn obedience when we suffer, just like Jesus did? Isn't that what He wanted us to understand? Amen, amen, I say to you, unless a grain of wheat falls to the ground and dies, it remains just a grain of wheat; but if it dies, it produces much fruit. (John 12:24) Do you struggle to understand why the pain and suffering?

Lord, I pray today that you help the people that are going through suffering, that You comfort them.

Hebrews 5: 7-9

March 23, 2015

Have you ever been in a situation where you felt helpless to the accusations that were being thrown at you? How did you react? The woman in this story was probably guilty as accused, but Jesus came to forgive sins, and let her go, telling her, "Neither do I condemn you. Go, and from now on do not sin any more". (John 8:11) Why do the accusers leave? What did Jesus write in the ground? It is thought that He wrote the sins of the accusers in the ground, and seeing their own sin, they knew they were not much better, so they left without throwing the stones. Maybe this is where the saying comes from that says, "Those who live in glass houses, should not throw stones". Are you an accuser? Are you without sin? Do you bring your sins to God? Do you continue to sin, knowing that God will forgive? Do you need forgiveness?

Lord, You probe me, and know me, may I live a life knowing Your forgiveness, and sin no more.

John 8:1-11

March 24, 2015

Is it possible to have food as something we idolize? What is your typical meal like? When I was younger, my dad used to say, "You don't eat to live, you live to eat". For the longest time I didn't realize how true that statement was. I do like food, and I like it tasty. But I never really thought about food being an idol. The Israelites were being provided food by God, when they were in the desert for 40 years, and they were complaining that they were tired of it. They wanted tasty food, not mana, and birds. They weren't happy with what they were provided, they wanted more. Do you appreciate what you have, or do you want something better, or what someone else has? Do you watch food shows, and want what they're having? How hard is it to be thankful for what you are given?

Lord, I thank You for everything you have provided for me. May I always remember that You have given it, and I should do the same.

Numbers 21:4-9

March 25, 2015

How likely are you to do what God asks of you? How quickly do you respond, when you are called? Today we recognize the announcement, to Mary of Jesus' conception. When the Angel Gabriel came to Mary to announce that she was to have a Son who is to be conceived of the Holy Spirit, she doesn't ask, "why me?", she asks how can this be, and accepts the responsibility. Maybe because an Angel spoke to her, she realized it must be so, but maybe she was brought up to always trust God, and be open to whatever God came to her with. She recognized the Angel. Do you know the angels that are in your life, and you always trust? How quick are you to say, "Yes Lord!"?

My God, and my Father, help me to see the clear signs of Your love for me, and trust in You, to accept all that You ask of me.

Luke 1:26-38

March 26, 2015

Have you ever thought about where you would have been, if you were living in Jesus' time, and in the same area? Would you have been on the side of the Pharisees, and other religious of the time, or would you have been following Jesus? Here was a man who had performed miracles, and healed people, and even raised people from the dead, and said He is the, "I Am", that you were taught all along, stood for God. Would you believe Him, or would you have been one of them throwing stones? He talked about not seeing death, yet we all know, everyone that has walked this earth has died. But have all had eternal death? The death we see, is only a passage from this life to the next, but where will it take you? Will it be with our Heavenly Father, or without Him, throwing stones? Do you believe Jesus is I AM?

Lord, through faith, You have saved me. May I be Your servant, and through my works, bring people to know You. Forgive me of my sins.

John 8:51-59

March 27, 2015

Have you wondered about the saying, "There's a time and place everything"? How many times do we hear about Jesus escaping the grasps, of those who wish to persecute Him? He always slips away, normally unscathed. When they came to get Him in the garden, He went willingly. Jesus points out the hypocrisy in the Jews trying to find reason to take Him in, by showing Him the works that He has done. They recognize the works, but focus on the words that He speaks. In this last few days before Easter, try to spend more time in prayer, and reflection. Are you doing things that help people see God, or are you doing things that make them question if there is a God? Are you true to God, and the people around you? Is it your time to speak up, and take action?

Lord, Your strength has carried me through the rough times, may I not disappoint You, even when I struggle through those difficulties. May those around me, see You, and not my weakness.

John 10:31-42

March 28, 2015

Does knowing that there is someone who can change your life, make you stronger, and make people not like you, make you want to change your life even more? There are people you call your friends, that would criticize you for believing, but does that scare you, or make you bolder? Why would they want to kill Jesus for performing miracles, and teaching what we should know? Is it because they would lose everything they were comfortable with? Were they so consumed with their own well-being, that they were willing to sacrifice a life for their own good? Would you sacrifice what you have, to have a life with purpose, or would you rather see that someone else give something, even a life, so that you may live? Will you pray all the way up to Easter, to have God guide you to understand why His Son had to die for you?

Lord, may I show the kind of love for my family, friends, and even those I have a hard time loving, Your loving mercy.

John 11:45-56

March 29, 2015

Are you influenced by peer pressure? A lot of people will say they are stronger than that, but when you are outnumbered, it is a lot harder to stand for what you believe. We live in a society where we are constantly bombarded with things that we need to accept, even if we don't like it. When Jesus came into Jerusalem, He was hailed "Hosanna! Blessed is he who comes in the name of the Lord! Blessed is the kingdom of our father David that is to come! Hosanna in the highest!"(Mark 11:9-10) The Jewish leaders had many opportunities to take Jesus, and failed, and part of the reason was because they feared the people that were following Him. So they concocted a plan that they could arrest Him in the middle of the night when no one was around. After they arrested Him, they incited the crowd to now chant, "Crucify Him". How did the people go from praise, to crucify, in less than a week? Was it peer pressure? Are we really that easily influenced? Are we that afraid of what people think of us, if we stand up for what we believe? Do you stand up for your faith, or do you join in, or ignore it? Who will be with you, when you are being crucified?

Lord, there is no guarantee that the people I call friends and family, will stand with me when I defend You, but I am always reassured that You will stand with me, and strengthen me.

Mark 11:1-10

March 30, 2015

Have you ever thought about why one of the 12 Apostles had to be the one that handed Jesus over to the Jews? Why wasn't it just one of the disciples that were following Jesus everywhere He went? Was Judas picked for that sole purpose, knowing that he was so money driven, that he would have no problem doing anything for money, even giving up someone who had showed him nothing but kindness all the time he was with him? You would think Jesus would have been aware of who Judas was. Did it have to be someone close to Jesus, so he would always know where he was? Maybe that information was not given to Jesus, until just before they celebrated the Passover together for the last time? Would you go out of your way to please God, or try to suppress what He has to say to the world?

Lord we may never know everything about You, but what You have revealed to me, has given me life and purpose.

John 12:1-11

March 31, 2015

Were you raised in a Christian home? Have you always believed? The contrast today, is Judas takes the morsel from Jesus, and the gospel of John says, "Satan entered him". Then we see Peter, who has followed on only his faith that Jesus is the Messiah, and we see that when he is tested, he denies even knowing Jesus. Judas was leaving, he just needed a little prodding. Peter was staying, but he needed to have someone point out that his faith wasn't where it needed to be yet. Sometimes we think we are aware of all that is Holy, but when push comes to shove, we will pick a side. Peter becomes one of the greatest witnesses to the life of Christ, and the Good News, because he wasn't shaken from his faith, he was strengthened by the challenge. Judas takes his own life into his own hands, and let's Satan take control. Have you been challenged? Have you just taken someone's word for your faith, and let little things weaken you, or do get stronger from the challenge? Will you stand with Christ, or hang with Judas?

Lord, so many times I am challenged, and You have carried me to know You deeper. May I be as faithful to You as You have been forgiving of me.

John 13:21-33, 36-38

April 1, 2015

Do you think of Jesus as your Lord, or is He just a prophet, or teacher? Yesterday in John's account, we see that Judas was the same as the rest of the Apostles, except Satan entered him. Today in Matthew's Gospel, we see that all the Apostles say, "Surely it is not I, Lord?"(Matthew 26:22), but when it is time for Judas, he says, "surely it is not I, Rabbi?"(Matthew 26:25) They all saw the same things, and heard the same things from Jesus, yet Judas only saw Jesus as a teacher, and the others saw Him as the Son of God. We all see things differently, and cannot all agree, because of our point of view, or our indoctrination. Are you open to knowing God more fully, or do you see things more skeptically, and need personal proof? If you witness a miracle, is it just a matter of circumstance, or is it Devine intervention? Is there anything that would make you believe, or change you, or is there nothing to be changed?

Lord, thank You for allowing me to see You more fully, and to know You are with me.

Matt 26:14-25

April 2, 2015

Have you ever wondered why Jesus came back into Jerusalem and what the Passover is? Take some time today and read Exodus 12:1-15. The Jewish people celebrated that God would allow them to live and bring them out of slavery from Egypt. They were told by God to celebrate this every year at the same time, to remember what God had done for them. In today's Gospel we see Jesus humbling himself, by washing the feet of the disciples. Why would He do that? Why weren't the disciples washing His feet, as they should? Why do we get so much satisfaction out of doing something for someone else, and helping them? Is He saying that, no matter how great you are, or think you are, you are nothing without serving others? Today is Holy Thursday, when Jesus gave us the understanding of Him giving us to eat, and drink His body and blood in the Holy Eucharist? Just like the Passover, God gave us a sign of His love for us. Do you know the love of God's mercy for us?

Thank you Lord for Your gift of Your Son, and all You have done for me.

John 13:1-15

April 3, 2015

What is truth? In today's reading from the Gospel of John, we hear Pilate ask, "What is Truth?" Have you ever personally read the passion of our Lord? Please take the time today to read it, and ask God to help you understand. Why did this have to happen? What else could have been done? Did God already try everything over the last thousands of years, and the people didn't understand? We are always searching, but are we looking for answers, where we should be? What is the meaning?

Thank You Lord for the sacrifice You made, to show Your forgiveness of my sins.

John 18:1—19:42

April 4, 2015

Do you wonder, after Jesus died on the cross, what He did? Did he just lay in the tomb awaiting that third day to fulfill the scripture prophecies? Did you know it's believed that He descended into Hell to save the souls that had died before Him? Some will have a hard time grasping that, but why wouldn't they also have a chance to be saved? Did he save all souls from Hell? Was He able to go where it is so dark that most people cannot fathom the evil that would be there? Would that deter Him? Take the time to reflect on your life, and pray for yourself. Do you ever pray for your own soul? Do you pray for others more?

Lord may I see You in others, and know that I am also in need of Your saving grace, and that I am never so far away from You that You can't save me.

Mark 16:1-7

April 5, 2015

When you hear that Jesus has been raised from the dead, do you run with joy to know more about it? When the disciples heard that Jesus was no longer in the tomb, they ran to see if it was true. After they saw He was no longer in the tomb, they were still not sure what that meant for them, but they were excited, and we will see in the next few days, still a little fearful. We are like that about our faith. We see others that have this joy, and share it with everyone they see, but we are still not sure if we are safe from persecution. We have no fear of speaking about Easter when it comes to the Easter bunny, but can we speak about our risen Lord as easily? Can you share this glorious news of our risen Lord?

Lord, by Your rising You have given us new life, and new hope. May Your blessings of love and forgiveness be with all this Easter season.

John 20:1-9

April 6, 2015

How easy is it for you to tell people something, different, when you don't understand what really happened? What would have happened if the guards would have went and told the story the way they saw it? Would the Jewish people now believe in the risen Lord? We hear later that many of the Romans started to believe. Did the guards help with that by telling their people what they saw? What if they went, as Roman guards, and told the truth to the world, would the world be a different place? They feared persecution. Do you also fear those who refuse to believe, because they can sometimes make you feel like you are brain washed? Do you believe what you have seen, and heard? If so, why not let people know?

Lord through the strength you have given me, and the courage of the Holy Spirit, may I be a witness to Your Holy name.

Matthew 28:8-15

April 7, 2015

What would it take to bring more than three thousand people together to hear someone speak? Even in today's world of technology, it is hard to get the attention of that many people long enough to interest them. Peter spoke with authority after seeing Jesus Christ risen from the dead. He spoke with purpose because his life seemed to, all of the sudden have real purpose. The people listened because he told them what had happened, and was fearless in doing so. Do you believe that the resurrection story can change lives that dramatically? Have you shared your faith story with anyone, much less the people that may need to hear some good news? We all have a story, but does anyone else know it? Do your friends know about the forgiveness that God has shown you?

Lord, may I take every opportunity to share the forgiveness You have shown me, and share the story of faith that has given my life purpose.

Acts 2:36-41

April 8, 2015

Have you ever watched a show, or movie, or read a book, and wondered what just happened, then you ask someone else, and they did the same thing, then you read what the writer had meant, and then you understand? The disciples all saw what was going on, and witnessed the brutality of Jesus' crucifixion, and even heard what Jesus was teaching them, yet they didn't get it. Sometimes we need the guidance of the writer, or the inspiration of the writer, to understand the story within the story. The disciples didn't even recognize Jesus was the one helping them understand, until He sat down and broke bread with them. Do you pray for guidance and understanding for what is happening to you? Do you look at your life as it has a God given purpose? What is God's plan for you?

Lord, so often I get so caught up in everything that is going on, that I forget, that it's not about me. Help me to see where you want to lead me.

Luke 24:13-35

April 9, 2015

Why does Jesus ask the disciples for something to eat? They gave Him a piece of fish to eat. It doesn't say they immediately recognized Him, but in other parts of the Gospel accounts it does. Why the food? Does food remove our anxiety, and bring us closer together? Does it help us to see more clearly? Think about the times when you gather as a family, and how everybody opens up to each other. We tend to share more openly. This last Easter Sunday, did you spend time with family? Did you get time to catch up on what was happening? Some people stress about getting together with family, and people like myself, relish in that time together. If you haven't spent time together with someone you care about, ask them to join you in a meal together, whether it is out to eat, or at your home. Can it heal a broken heart, or maybe even a relationship? Will you see something new in that person that you have not seen before?

Lord, open my eyes to see You, and know You in those around me, and in the time we spend together.

Luke 24:35-48

April 10, 2015

Are you confident when being persecuted? Do you stand up for what is right, and accuse the accusers of their hypocrisy? I love the Acts of the Apostles. They feared nothing because they knew God was on their side, and the Holy Spirit was alive in them. The leaders of the Jewish community were accusing them of healing a man (they were doing something good), and they were doing it in the name of Jesus Christ. They didn't like this, because it showed a wrong that they had done, and couldn't get away from. Sometimes it is kind of an, "in your face", bold way to confront, but sometimes, that is the only way. Do you truly believe that Jesus Christ was crucified, died, and was buried, and then rose from the dead? If you do, why is it so hard to stand up for our Christianity? Will you be bold in the face of persecution, and confront the attacker? Do you believe, and follow?

Lord, I know You are with me, and my strength comes from Your Holy Spirit, may I be as strong as Your Apostles when faced with persecution.

Acts 4:1-12

April 11, 2015

Do you wait for God to come to you, or are you like Mary Magdalene and go to Him, even in the face of danger? Mary loved Jesus because He had done so much for her, by casting out the demons. She wanted nothing but to serve Jesus. The Apostles feared the Jewish leaders who had persecuted Jesus, and were hiding. They would not even believe it when they were told that Jesus had been raised from the dead, just as He said he would. Does the fear overcome you so much that you need to see to believe? Do you have the faith needed to witness, or are you waiting for Jesus to walk up to you and be physically present? What is faith? Is it trusting in what you have been told, and heard, or is it seeing to believe? Isn't seeing and believing, just sharing? How strong is your faith?

Lord I know the persecutors will challenge me because they need to see to believe. Help me to be strong, when I am weak in my faith.

Mark 16:9-15

April 12, 2015

Have you figured out what truth is? Remember back on Good Friday, we heard Pilate ask, "What is truth?", when speaking with Jesus? The first letter of John 5:6 says, "The Spirit is the one that testifies, and the Spirit is truth." In today's Gospel reading, we hear about doubting Thomas, one of the Apostles that said He would not believe unless he saw Jesus before him. The Apostles had not yet received the Holy Spirit, and therefore faith was hard for them. They were all still hiding behind locked doors, afraid of being persecuted. Don't we also have a hard time speaking about our faith, and believing, because we have not seen? If we have faith and we believe without seeing, Jesus says we are blessed. Jesus breathed the Holy Spirit on the Apostles, and they went out proclaiming the Good News without fear of persecution. "What is truth?" you ask? It is the Holy Spirit in us that gives us the faith we need. Do you trust that same Holy Spirit lives in you?

Lord, by faith I trust in You, may I be so bold as to speak Your Holy name, and not fear persecution, and if it comes, may my faith never waiver, because You have given me TRUTH.

John 20:19-31

April 13, 2015

After Lent and Easter, have you changed anything in your life, to give you a renewed spirit? Nicodemus came to Jesus in the evening, when there were very few people around. He wanted to talk, and acknowledge that he realized Jesus was from God. Then Jesus tells him he needs to be born from above, in order to see the Kingdom of God (John 3:3). This statement is very puzzling to Nicodemus, because he doesn't know how to reenter the womb. So many times we hear God speaking to us, and we either choose to not believe, or we just don't understand. We go through Lent every year to help us understand God more deeply, and His will for us, but do we truly want to be born into the spirit? Sometimes it sounds good, but we very seldom want our old self to die. We've become comfortable with that person that has made us, even though something inside us knows we need to be better, and die to our old self. Will you allow the Spirit to move through you, even though you don't know where He will take you?

Lord, I know I can be better. May I allow Your Spirit to guide me, and may I follow, knowing that it is always for the better.

John 3:1-8

April 15, 2015

What would it be like in this world, if there were no Christians, or anybody with a hint of love for God? Would it be chaos? Would it be Hell? Have you ever gone into a cave, far enough to not be able to see even a hint of light, and distinguish all light sources? This is a new kind of darkness. You can't even see your hand before your face. I'm not sure that even night vision goggles would work there. If you were left there without a light source, you could potentially never get out, depending on the cave. It is even colder in caves, because of the lack of light. That is what our life is like when we do not have a presence of God. There are some that will say they live a life without God, but I say, if there were nobody around you that had some faith in God, your life would most likely be miserable. Jesus Christ is our light source, and gives us the vision to see, and the comfort of warmth, in knowing we're cared for. No matter how little we keep Him in our hearts, His light will shine through, and provide light for others, to see. Will you allow Christ's presence to shine through you today, and make someone else's life a little better, and help them see?

Lord Jesus Christ, You are the source of all that is good in this world, May I never fear or waiver in shining Your light, so others may see more clearly, and feel the warmth of Your presence.

John 3:16-21

April 16, 2015

What's the difference between witnessing something, and telling about it, and hearing the story, and telling about it? When you witness something, don't you speak with authority, and conviction because you know all the details? When someone tells you the story, isn't it hard to repeat it with authority because it is hard to remember everything? The Apostles were boldly telling people about Jesus, and what they had witnessed because they witnessed it, and the Holy Spirit was in them. They had no reason to fear man, because they knew what they witnessed was not from man, it was from God. Man could not make them stop, because they were telling the facts about what happened, and what they witnessed. Would they have been so bold standing up against the people wanting to imprison or kill them, if they had not been part of what had happened? The Holy Spirit was in them, the same way He is in us who believe. Are you bold enough to witness what has been written, or do you fear people who don't believe? If you haven't read the Acts of the Apostles, I strongly encourage you to take the time to read what the Apostles did, after they witnessed Jesus' resurrection.

Oh Holy Spirit, with You I am stronger than those who wish to persecute me. May I speak as a witness to what I know, and have read?

Acts 5:27-33

April 17, 2015

Why is it that most people, when they die, they take their legacy with them? Do you ever wonder, "Who will attend my funeral, when I pass?" We all try to make a difference in this world, and want to make our mark, but will anyone care after we have been gone? We try to do things that people will remember us for, good, or bad. The life that Jesus lived was truly remarkable, and probably would have lived in the memories of those that met Him, or knew Him, until they died, but He isn't remembered, for all time, simply for the life He lived, but for what happened after He died. He gave the people that knew Him purpose to live, by rising from the dead, and giving them the Holy Spirit. His legacy did not die, because it is from God, and God does not die. The Pharisees knew that if they leave the disciples of Jesus alone, this would all pass, if it wasn't from God. Will you be remembered for what you did for people, or will you be remembered for eternity, for what you do for God?

Lord, Your life, and Your resurrection gives me purpose, may I do as You ask of me, for Your Glory.

Acts 5:34-42

April 18, 2015

Why do we forget so easily, the good things that happen in our lives, and panic so quickly when something is unfamiliar to us? The disciples had just witnessed Jesus feeding 5,000 people with a couple fish and a few loaves of bread. They go to the other side of the sea to relax, and when they see someone walking across the water, they panic, until Jesus tells them it is Him. Did they think He was a ghost? Do we so fear the unknown that we think anything that is unfamiliar has to be bad? How hard is it for you to see the good in a situation rather than the bad? Do you have the faith to trust that even what is unfamiliar can be something good?

My God, and Father, may I have the faith to know You are always with me, and even what I don't understand You are there.

John 6:16-21

April 19, 2015

Why do most of us fear sharing the Good News of Jesus Christ dying for our sins? Most of us fear what other people think of us more than what God thinks of us. The disciples were walking on the road, after they had already seen Jesus risen from the dead, and still were in disbelief. Jesus has to help them understand what happened and why it had to happen. He even asked if they needed to touch His wounds, to believe. He told them, "You are witnesses of these things"(Luke 24:48). Why would He say that? Isn't He telling them to witness to what they saw, by making that statement? Why would all this happen, if it wasn't for us to make sure everyone knows about His death, and resurrection, for our sins? What do you need to convince you to share the Good News of forgiveness, and Jesus' resurrection?

Lord may You open the eyes of your faithful, and give them the courage to speak in Your Holy name, to share Your love for us.

Luke 24:35-48

April 20, 2015

Have you ever noticed when a person has changed their life around? We see it all the time in people we knew long ago, and see again for the first time in years. You notice something different in them, but you're not really sure what it is. Sometimes people change overnight, and you don't understand it. Sometimes you want to ask them the same thing the disciples asked Jesus, "When did you get here?(John 6:25) What changed in their life? Is it a more caring person? Is it someone who barely talked or socialized, and now they are very open and social? Is it someone who lived a different lifestyle than you're comfortable with, and now they have changed? Jesus does not answer the question, He tells them, and they are looking for something to fill the place they know needs to be filled. We don't always know what that is, but God is the only thing that can fill that emptiness. Even people that do not believe in God, are looking for something to fill an emptiness in their life. When we find how God can fill our lives with purpose, we change, and people ask, "When did you get here?" Are you still searching for a life of purpose? Have you heard how God can change lives? Do you have an emptiness in your life?

Lord, You have filled my life with more than I could have ever expected. May You continue to show me new life.

John 6:22-29

April 21, 2015

How quickly have you seen lives changed? Stephen was not one of the original disciples, at least he was not mentioned as one, and he is the first recorded martyr, after Jesus gave them the Holy Spirit. He was so influenced by what he was told, and what the Holy Spirit gave him the strength for, that he spoke against what was happening, and how wrong they were in persecuting Jesus. He was willing to give his life for God, and what was right. He did not even wish vengeance on those that were persecuting, and killing him. He said," Lord, do not hold this sin against them"(Acts 7:60). We are also introduced to a man named Saul, at the end of this reading. Saul was leading the persecution of the newly found Christian church, and he would become one of the most noted writers in the Bible, as Paul. Can God change your life? Are you comfortable with that kind of change? How will that change the way you live?

Lord, many times I have seen You work in other people, and I am in awe of the great works you can perform with the people You have chosen. May Your love continue to change lives, and give them purpose.

Acts 7:51—8:1a

April 22, 2015

Do you have to see something to believe it? The 6th Chapter of John is one of the most fascinating of all the Bible. This is John's discourse on Jesus' teaching on the bread of life. Jesus tells the crowd that everyone who sees Him, and believes in Him will have eternal life, and be raised on the last day. How do we see Jesus, if He is in Heaven? Where is He present for us to see Him? We say that we see Him in the people around us, but is that what He meant? Later in this chapter, we find that Jesus tells the people He is the bread of life, and we must eat His body and drink His blood. This so disturbed some of the disciples that they left Him. Is that also disturbing to you? We see in all the readings about His last supper, that He takes the bread, and says, "This is my Body which will be given up for you", and likewise, He takes the cup, and says, "This is the blood of the new covenant that will be poured out for you"(Mathew 26:26-27). Do we see Jesus in the bread, and the wine after consecration, and truly eat the body of Christ and drink His blood? This is some very profound teaching, and a core of what the Catholic Church teaches. There is plenty of material, that supports this teaching, and yes you will find some that rebuts it, but I challenge you to do your own research, and pray as you do, that the Holy Spirit help you understand. Will you see Jesus, and believe, or is this teaching so hard that you will follow the disciples that left Jesus?

Lord, Your teaching are hard for us who have not been a part of Your physical life, but thankfully You have provided the Holy Spirit to guide our ways and our thoughts.

John 6:35-40

April 23, 2015

How willing are you to jump up and go do something that the Holy Spirit has told you to do? Is the angel of the Lord and the Holy Spirit the same? Philip does not ask why he was told to go to Gaza, on the desert route, he just gets up and goes. No question. He knew who was talking to him. Then he's told to join the chariot. He's not told to go speak to the eunuch about who Jesus is, but he knows God sent him here for a reason. Do you know why you are where you are? Has God put you there for a reason? We leave jobs, we move to different towns, we are surrounded by people that want to talk, about something. What do you talk about? Most everybody will talk about the weather but, sometimes it seems that even the weatherman doesn't know anything about the weather, and yet we say we don't want to talk about God, because we don't know enough. The Holy Spirit is always with us, we need only to ask for His wisdom and guidance. If you heard the angel of the Lord speaking to you, would you listen, and do what He asks? Do you know His voice?

Lord, show me the way! May I go where You ask, and know You are with me always.

Acts 8:26-40

April 24, 2015

Have you ever been blindsided, and had no idea what was going to happen next? Saul was arresting and having put to death anyone who belonged to "The Way", Christians. This was anyone who proclaimed Christ crucified and resurrected. He was knocked from his horse and blinded, and when he asked who was speaking to him everyone nearby heard Jesus' voice. We talk about knowing and recognizing the Holy Spirit speaking to us, but no one else probably hears that voice. There was no doubt in Saul's mind what had just happened, and he did what he was guided to do. The name Saul would leave him, and he would now be known as Paul, the author of most of the letters in the New Testament of the Bible, and one of the greatest evangelists of all time. How bad is your life? What have you done that God can forgive you for? Can He use you, just as He used Saul/Paul? Are you willing?

Lord, no matter my faults, You can use me, and I offer You my life, to use as You know wish.

Acts 9:1-20

April 25, 2015

What does it mean to be sober and vigilant? Doesn't sober mean, to be alert to what is happening around you? Doesn't vigilant mean to be persistent? Why would we have to be that way? What are we to worry about? Some people will deny the devil even exists. Is it because they don't want to believe in the spiritual warfare that is always going on? Do they not want to admit that there is the possibility that they may not make it to Heaven? Why do some people give up on life, and let the devil devour their soul, and lose that spiritual war? "The God of all grace who called you to his eternal glory through Christ Jesus will himself restore, confirm, strengthen, and establish you after you have suffered a little" (1 Peter 5:10). Will you be sober and vigilant in knowing that God will protect you, and save you from the evil that awaits those who let down their guard?

Lord, grant me the strength to be humble in the face of adversity, and not let my pride overcome me.

1 Peter 5:5b-14

April 26, 2015

How much do you love your children? Most good parents will say they love their children enough that they would lay down their life for them. How about someone else's children, would you lay down your life for them? Some of us would do that. What if your child has done things that makes you proud, would you still give your life for theirs? What if your child doesn't want to acknowledge you, will you still die for them? What about a family member, does that make a difference? We put conditions on life when their ways don't agree with our ways. But the good parent will always sacrifice their life for their child's life, no matter the condition. Jesus didn't lay down His life, just for the people that have not sinned. He died for all of us, whether we accept Him or not. It is not conditional, His life was sacrificed for sinners, and good people alike. Do you know that kind of love? Isn't that what unconditional love is?

Thank you Jesus for the love you have poured for ALL Your people, may I share that love with those I come in contact with.

John 10:11-18

April 27, 2015

Have you ever watched animated movies, and tried to figure out who the actors are, that are playing the parts of the characters? All you get is the voice, no visual of the person. Every voice has a distinct tone or pitch, and if you listen, you can tell who is reading the part. We recognize voices that we are familiar with, and they bring out a certain feeling for the character. I think of the unique voices like Robin Williams. We recognize his immediately, and associate his character with what we remember of him. Sheep recognize the Shepard of their flock in the same way. They know the voice, and will not follow anyone except their Shepard, because they know he provides for them, and will not harm them. He will lead them to food and comfort. Jesus has shown us the way to Heaven, and leads us. We need only to trust Him, and follow Him. Do you know His voice? Have you been led astray, and are reluctant to follow, because you no longer know His voice? How will you know His voice? Spend some time in His word, the Bible, and get to know Him, and you will recognize His voice.

Lord, I know You have seen the ones who have lost their way, and no longer know Your voice, may You open their hearts to hear You again.

John 10:1-10

April 28, 2015

Have you ever tried showing someone God's love, and what Jesus has done for us? We struggle sometimes, because we want them to know who Jesus is, and yet they see the world around them, and can't see what Jesus taught, or His miracles. We should never feel like it is our fault for not being able to save a soul. We can only plant seeds, and occasionally water the ground. Only God can give them sight, and help them understand. Jesus was right in front of people performing miracles, and the Apostles were first hand witnesses to Jesus' life and resurrection, and they still could not convince everyone. Does that mean we shouldn't try? If we see someone struggling should we just turn our backs and walk away? Can't we at least help them to know the voice of the Shepard when He speaks to them? If you know His voice, shouldn't you help other people recognize it also?

Lord so many times I have heard You calling, and have tried to go the other way, may I know Your voice and say, "here I am Lord, it is I Lord", and follow You.

John 10:22-30

April 29, 2015

Did you know that a lot of people that don't believe in Jesus Christ as our Lord and Savior, don't believe because it was written by man? Isn't there something really strange about that? Usually that thought process was put there by man, but yet they believe that. They use that same argument when it comes to the history of our nation, when it is something they don't want to believe. How do you justify anything then, unless you personally witness it? Jesus didn't come to condemn those who do not believe that He is the light, but that disbelief will affect how they are judged on the last day. Jesus is the light that guides us, and makes us see the things that some choose not to see. Do you use Jesus as your guiding light to see the world for what it is, and God for who He is? Do you believe because you have seen the light, or do you see the light because you believe?

Lord Jesus Your light guides me where I am to go and gives my life purpose, may I trust in Your word above the worldly things that distract, and be guided by that light.

John 12:44-50

April 30, 2015

What does it mean to be betrayed by someone you specifically selected to be by your side? Jesus chose Judas to be a part of His "team", to show the world how much God loved them. Judas must have become disoriented with all that was going on, and started to wonder, "is He really the king we are waiting for?" People today, that have once followed Jesus, have left Him because they too have had doubts about "what is truth?" There is so much that we see with all the information, at our hands. When someone says something, you can search it in minutes on a smart phone. It is betrayal to know God, and at some point, decide that maybe these other people are right, when they say, "this God is not what I was looking for". God's love knows no bounds, unlike our human self, that when we see something we don't understand, we don't try to find out more, we just give up on it. We need direction, and unfortunately, there is also a lot of misdirection available also. How deep is your love and understanding? If someone comes along and argues their point, do you give up on what you know to be true? Have you given up on God? You know He will never give up on you.

Lord, when I struggle with the things I don't understand, help me to see with Your eyes, that I may know You more deeply, so that when the challenges come, my heart will know.

John 13:16-20

May 1, 2015

Have you ever had to go somewhere and maps and GPS systems couldn't get you to where you wanted to go, so you got to the area, and had to ask a local? The people that are familiar with the town know the way, because they live there, and have been to the place you're looking for. Why do the maps and GPS not get you to the proper place? Is it because they don't know the town, they just have information that was provided to them? Don't we also wonder if we are heading in the right direction, when it comes to our own salvation? Once we get close, it seems we still are a little lost, because we're not quite there yet. We know Jesus is the way, but the world still makes us doubt. We tend to put our trust in others, more than in God. Jesus tells His disciples, "I am the way and the truth and the life. No one comes to the Father except through me."(John 14:6), and we still wonder if we are there. Do you know Jesus? How hard is it for you to spend a little time in the scriptures, and get to know Him? Isn't that how we get to know more about someone, or some place, we spend time there?

Lord, may I know You more deeply, and understand You more fully, so I can help others that need direction.

John 14:1-6

May 2, 2015

How often are your prayers answered? Are they answered, but not the way you wanted them answered? Did you pray in Jesus' name when you prayed? Jesus says, "And whatever you ask in my name, I will do, so that the Father may be glorified in the Son. If you ask anything of me in my name, I will do it."(John 14:13-14) How many times have you asked something, and it did not happen? We pray, and we hope, but do we pray and believe that if we ask it in Jesus' name, it will happen? Are you confident in knowing that your prayers will be answered? When our girls were younger, we played a lot of games, and Cassy kept beating me in a card game. I asked her if she was cheating, and she said, "No". I asked how she kept beating me, and she said, "She kept praying for better cards". I almost told her it didn't work that way, but did she believe more than I did? How about when we ask for healing? We have all prayed for the healing of ourselves, or a loved one, and sometimes, it just isn't meant to be. Would that healing alter God's ultimate plan for us? What if that illness was to make our prayer life stronger, or help someone else through a difficult time? What do you ask of God, in Jesus' name?

My God and my Father, may I have the faith and trust in You to ask and receive, in the name of Your Holy Son, Jesus Christ.

John 14:7-14

May 3, 2015

Why would Jesus use a vine and branches to teach His disciples? Is it because the pruning that needs to be done to each of us? Is it to remind us that we can't do it on our own? This teaching is fascinating because it is short, and there are multiple things to take from it. We cannot produce fruit, if we are separated from Jesus, and when we do produce fruit, we are still going to be pruned, so that we can produce more. When a tree or vine gets pruned, it has the pain of loss, but it is to allow it to produce more fruit. We all experience loss in our lives, of friends, and family, and we can either cut ourselves off from God because of the pain we are experiencing, or we can see the good that comes from that loss, and produce more fruit than we thought possible. The pain is difficult, but we can choose how we handle that pain. Do you remain in Christ, or do you disconnect? Jesus says, "I am the vine, you are the branches. Whoever remains in me and I in him will bear much fruit, because without me you can do nothing."(John 15:5) How do you deal with the pruning of your life?

Lord grant me your strength, in times of pruning, that I may grow, and produce more fruit. May I be always a branch of Your love.

John 15:1-8

May 3, 2015 (part 2)

Yes this is the second one today, and it is long. Sorry for that, but the message is important.

Have you ever moved to a different town, different school, or different job? Some of you know me as family, relative, friend, teacher, co-worker, and even coach. Some know me from when I was a lot younger, and some have only had brief times of discussion with me. Some don't really know me, but because it is so easy to be a "friend" on Facebook, we have connected there. I have shared some deep things with you, and some funny things, but you may still wonder, who I am. When I moved to Cumberland, WI when I was 14, it was the custom to have a student the same age, take you around school and introduce you to other kids, and teachers. I was fortunate to have Robert Cifaldi do the task. Bob didn't know me from Adam, and yet he did what any good person would do. He took me under his wing, and became a friend to me, without knowing me. We have become better friends over the years, and I have bought a few cars from him. If he had to introduce me now, he would probably do nothing different. Barnabas had the task of introducing Paul, and bringing him into the group of disciples, knowing that they feared him, because they knew him as someone who was persecuting anyone who taught Jesus' lifesaving message. Paul had changed, and they still feared him, because, "was he still the murderer they had all heard about?" What is it like to change your life for something with purpose, when you thought you were fulfilling your destiny before? Do you know your purpose in this life? Have you altered your life to be better? Do you work your job, or go to school because you have to, or is your job, and school the vehicle you use to fulfill God's plan?

Lord, may You continue to change me to be who You desire.

Acts 9:26-31

May 4, 2015

Have you ever watched a show, or movie with someone else, and they figured out what was going on before you did, or vise a versa? When we watch, we don't always pay attention to all the details, even though we are focused on the same thing, figuring it out. Why do you suppose that is? Is it because our interests are different, so we see things with a different light? Ask three people who witness the same thing, and they will all tell you similar things but different details. What are our interests? What do we see? Is it what we want to see? How often do you want to understand more, and actually ask the Holy Spirit to help you see, and understand? When you pray, ask that you are able to see as God sees, so that you will see what is important. God doesn't want you to not see, He wants you to see as He sees. Do you want to see as God sees, or is life easier, not seeing some things? Are you worried that if you see differently, it will change you, and you don't like change?

Holy Spirit, open my eyes to see You, in all that I am a part of. May that vision allow me to know You more fully.

John 14:21-26

May 5, 2015

What does persistence and determination look like? If you have a reason to carry on, isn't persistence and determination easy? If you find purpose, the body and the spirit can withstand a lot. If you have the chance to read "Lone Survivor", or "Unbroken", I strongly recommend them. Both of these men show the same kind of determination and will, as Paul does, to get through whatever it takes, to accomplish who they are, and what they live for. They have purpose. They have reason to not give up. Paul shows that, even though the same people he used to be part of, are trying to kill Him for his teachings, and belief, he will not give up. He has purpose and the knowledge that, this is what he has been placed here for, and it gives him reason to live. His life has purpose. Do you know what it is, to know your purpose, and reason for being? Does it involve something bigger than yourself? I encourage you to spend some time in silent prayer, to know who you really are, and your purpose.

Lord, walk with me this day, and help me to see what you have called me to be, and let me know if I am where You need me to be.

Acts 14:19-28

May 6, 2015

Why do we prune trees and vines? What good is a dead branch? Can it ever start re-growing fruit? If you trim back the bad, doesn't that give room for the good to grow? Isn't that a lot like our lives? Don't we have to remove what is not good for us, in order for the good in us to flourish? When I was young, I used to like to fight, because we were taught how to fight. Our dad didn't want us to be boys that couldn't defend ourselves, or our sister, not that Nadine needed a lot of help. I could not get away from the fighting because people knew I fought, and they would push me to the point, that I would fight. I was fortunate to have a place to move to, to get away from that reputation. I had to remove that part of me, and start over. It gave me new life, and room to grow. What in your life needs to be pruned in order for the good in you to flourish? Are you willing, and strong enough, to remove that from your life?

Lord, You have guided me to where I am, by removing the parts of me that did not allow growth, may You continue to prune me, that I may continue to produce fruit.

John 15:1-8

May 7, 2015

Are there any commandments that you have a hard time keeping? What about the two great commandments? How do you do with, love God with all your heart, all your mind, all your body and all your soul? That one seems easier than, love your neighbor as yourself. We have a hard time loving all our neighbors, because we know them. We know who they are, what they have done, and sometimes we don't like what they do. Sometimes, the more you know someone, the harder it is to love them. How well do you love yourself? I have always thought, this is what makes us be able to love someone else. How hard is it to love others, when you really don't love yourself? I'm not talking about people that are obsessed with themselves, I'm not sure there is enough for others when they obsess over themselves. Do you accept other people for who they are, and love them for who they are, even if they do not believe the way you believe? What is your definition of love?

Lord, help me to look past the things that are hard for me to accept, and see that they are still part of Your plan for our understanding, and love.

John 15:9-11

May 8, 2015

How hard would it be to die for someone? As a parent you're pretty sure you would do it for your kids. How about a sibling, a parent, or a friend? Some of us can fathom that, but what about someone you don't know? Jesus teaches us that, this is what true love is, to lay down your life for a friend. A friend is someone you know, and probably pretty well. Because Jesus lay down His life for all, wouldn't we all be His friends? He says "to love one another as I love you"(John 15:12). He doesn't say, "As I have loved you". It's not over. He doesn't stop loving us. Sometimes people feel they can no longer be loved by anyone else, even God, because of what we have done, but God still loves us. He may not like what you are doing, or have done, but He doesn't stop loving us. Has someone wronged you in this life that you have a hard time forgiving? For your own good, can you figure out how to forgive them? Are you capable of that kind of love?

Lord grant me the strength to go to those who have wronged me and offer them forgiveness, so that I may have a deeper understanding of Your love.

John 15:12-17

May 9, 2015

How many times have you wondered, "I'm a Christian, why am I being persecuted? Doesn't God love me?" Why do we think we should not have to go through trials in our lives just because we are Christians? We profess to follow Christ, and He even told us that we will be persecuted for our beliefs, yet we still don't understand. Why should it be any easier on us? Whoever said it would be easy? We have to choose between Christ and the world. As easy as some of us think this is, our kids are in school and college, and work, where sometimes they are belittled for believing in a God, and especially a risen Christ. Are you of this world, or are you strong enough to withstand the attacks on who you are? Or, is it easier for you to sit it out, and let others decide your fate? Jesus said, "If the world hates you, realize that it hated me first"(John 15:18). Will you stand with God, or without Him? It is your choice, you know, and it is not always the easy path. What fun is the easy path? Don't we thrive on challenges?

My Lord Jesus, be with me during the times I struggle to profess Your name, may Your strength and determination be what carries me through the tough times.

John 15:18-21

May 10, 2015

What is love? Most of us think we know it, and when we were younger maybe misunderstood it. As we age, we define love differently, because we have probably experienced a different kind of love, than we may have known when we were younger. When we are younger, the closest we can relate to real love, is the love of a caring and loving parent. We are not always blessed with that parent, but most will recognize that love, as we get older, and sometimes after the parent is gone, we realize the emptiness of the love we once knew. Being a parent, is sometimes the best example we can use to define love. Most will say they love their parents, and want to spend time with them, but when it comes down to it, how hard do you try? As someone who has lost both parents at a fairly young age, you realize there were opportunities that were missed, because you thought you could make it up. As a child, you have the opportunity to return the love to your parents, by spending time with them. Spend some time with your parents today, and show the appreciation of your love. Do you know the kind of love God has poured out for you?

Lord, today we recognize our mothers on this Mother's Day, may You bless each one of them with a love that knows no bounds, that they may share that love with their children. Thank you, for the mothers who have gone to see You, that we miss this day.

1 John 4:7-10

May 11, 2015

Have you ever wondered why "radical Muslims" will justify killing Christians and non-believers, and claim they are called by God to do so? This reading from the Gospel of John will shed some light on that. Did you know that Islam and Judaism, therefore Christian also, all point back to Abraham as the father of their faith? Islam traces back to Abraham's son Ishmael from the slave Hagar, and Christians and Jews trace back to Isaiah from Abraham's wife Sarah. We share the same God, and yet some believe it is in the name of God that they inflict death. Is this because they do not know Jesus in the Holy Spirit? Doesn't the Holy Spirit guide us, and give us understanding? Is that the difference? We know the Holy Spirit through Baptism, and then more deeply through Confirmation. Do you trust that the same Holy Spirit will give you the strength and wisdom to withstand the persecution from those that claim to know the same God? If you read the first book of the Bible, Genesis chapters 11-25, you get some history into why we are where we are, and the New Testament will give you the hope and understanding of Jesus' teaching and the gift of the Holy Spirit. Do you trust the Holy Spirit?

Lord Jesus, through Your teaching and with the guidance of Your Holy Spirit, we can stand in the face of persecution. May I be always faithful to You.

John 15:26—16:4a

May 12, 2015

What happens when you pray? Do you have earth shaking results? Many times we hope for that, just to be reminded God is there. Paul and Silas were preaching God's word, and the authorities had them beaten and arrested. Did they give up because they thought God gave up on them? No, they prayed all the more. Then the earth shook, and their chains fell off. God didn't say go free, he brought them the jailer that was responsible for keeping them locked up, and they saved the jailers life. Not only did they save Him, they went to his family and baptized the whole family. When God performs miracles in our lives, we sometimes think it was all about us, and thank God for that miracle, but most times that miracle was to give us hope, and encouragement to carry on. There are bigger things out there, than ourselves, we just need to see them. If you were Paul and Silas, would you have thanked God for freeing you, and then run, or would you have waited to see what God truly had planned for you? Do you understand the results of your prayers?

Lord, when I feel like giving up, and that I'm not doing enough good, help me to see where I can serve You even more. May I always know Your will for me, and trust You.

Acts 16:22-34

May 13, 2015

Can you bear the truth? It seems we all want to know what truth is. In today's reading from the Gospel of John, we see Jesus telling the disciples that they cannot bear the truth, so He will send the advocate, the Holy Spirit. So many times we overlook the Holy Spirit, and don't realize that He is here for us, to teach us the truth. He speaks what Jesus tells Him to speak, and only when we can bear it. We think we want to know more, but sometimes we are not ready for it. When I started in the Deacon training classes, there were things they were teaching us that made me get headaches, because I couldn't handle it at the time. There is some very deep theology, and I try to keep things simple, because, I am a simple man. Do you ask the Holy Spirit to help you understand things that just don't seem to make any sense?

Come, Holy Spirit, fill the hearts of Your faithful and kindle in them the fire of Your love. Send forth Your Spirit and they shall be created and You shall renew the face of the earth. O God, who taught the hearts of the faithful by the light of the Holy Spirit, grant that, by the same Holy Spirit, we may be truly wise, and ever rejoice in His consolation. Through Christ our Lord. Amen.

John 16:12-15

May 14, 2015

Do you do as Jesus commanded you to do? Do you proclaim the Gospel to every creature? He didn't "ask" us to do it, did He? Why do we fear proclaiming the Gospel? Do we fear being challenged by someone that may know more than we do? Remember this, there is always someone out there that may know, or claim to know, more than we do. This past few days and weeks we have been hearing a lot about the Holy Spirit. Isn't that what He was sent for, to give us knowledge, and wisdom, and courage, when we are speaking of the Gospel? Why do we have a tough time trusting in Him? You don't have to go out and stand on a street corner, and thump your Bible, there are already people that don't fear doing that. You just need to be tuned into the people and conversations around you. When you start paying attention, you find that there are a lot of opportunities to speak about things you know, and don't be afraid to ask for the guidance of the Holy Spirit before you speak. Will you be recognized by Jesus, and others, as one of His disciples? Will you be, His hero? (Sorry, I couldn't resist!)

My God and my Father, You have shown me how to overcome the fear and anxiety of speaking when I don't feel like the best person to share your word, may I always trust in Your Holy Spirit to guide my words.

Mark 16: 15-20

May 15, 2015

How often do you need extra encouragement? Sometimes we feel like we need it every day, sometimes we need it when we have had a rough time. Paul had already been going to the people and proclaiming the Good News for a few years, so he knew what he was to say, and that people were still trying to persecute him, but he still needed to be told, "Go, and don't be afraid". We all need to be encouraged occasionally, to at least reinforce our confidence. Most people think, if they're not in a leadership role, it is not their duty to encourage, but as someone who has been owner, manager, and laborer, I can tell you there are people that over encourage, and there are people that don't know the words. How hard is it for you to give someone a pat on the back for a job well done? Do you do it so often, that people don't believe it anymore? Go! make a difference!

Lord, Your life, and the lives of Your Apostles gives me the strength a courage to know that you never leave me. May I also be words of encouragement when I see someone who is giving up?

Acts 18:9-18

May 16, 2015

How often do you pray? Do you pray in the morning, and when you go to bed, or do you pray more often than that? When you pray, do you pray in the name of Jesus Christ? Does Jesus tell us to ask God in His name so we can affirm to God that we know His Son? As Catholics, we start our prayers, and end our prayers, by saying, "in the name of the Father, and the Son, and the Holy Spirit", while making the sign of the cross, to acknowledge that we know all three, and that we also acknowledge the cross. Sometimes people know Catholics by that simple gesture. It's not to draw attention, it is that simple acknowledgement. Will you ask in Jesus' name, with confidence?

Lord, Heavenly Father, may I always trust that You love me, and that I know You more deeply, because of Your Son, Jesus Christ.

John 16:23b-28

May 17, 2015

Do you proclaim the Gospel to the world? Do you believe? Have you been baptized? We fear so many things in this world, partly because we're unfamiliar with the possible outcome, or uncertainty of what people will think of us. Proclaiming the Gospel can be very intimidating at times, because there are people out there that probably know it better than us, but should we let that bother us? We need only trust that God is with us, in the form of the Holy Spirit. What more could we ask for? Shouldn't that give us the confidence we need? Do we not trust that He will really be with us? Ask any one of the people that question some of the content of these reflections. I don't always know the answers, but I am not doing this on my own. The answers come through the Holy Spirit guiding my words. Do you feel like you can perform miracles by proclaiming the Gospel? Do you want to? Do you fear it, or do you feel you aren't worthy? Miracles abound, we just need to open our eyes to see them, and sometimes be part of them.

Lord, when I feel weak, You give me strength through Your Holy Spirit, may I accept that strength, and not fear the world.

Mark 16: 15-20

May 18, 2015

What does Jesus mean when He says He has conquered the world? Don't we still see the violence that is from humankind? Don't we still see the evil that man can do to man? Did He take away our ability to have a free will? No! Did He take away the evil from the world? No! How then, did He conquer the world? The sin we see is still in the world, and there are still people that thrive on that evil. He gave us the ability to repent and receive the forgiveness that is from Him. That is forgiveness for the mistakes, and bad choices we do make. The world wants to make people believe they are condemned to Hell, and Jesus gives us the redemption that is from the cross and resurrection. He has conquered the lie of the world, we just need to know that He is the way of truth, and follow Him. We still have to choose to, either follow Jesus, who conquered the world, or deny Him, and be condemned with the world. For some it seems like an easy choice, for some, they have doubts. Can you help them know the true love of God through Jesus Christ?

Thank you Lord for the forgiveness You have poured out in all of us. May I take your saving grace to the world?

John 16:29-33

May 19, 2015

Will you have regrets for the life you have lived? Will you look back at some point and realize there are a lot of things you could have done differently for God's great glory? Paul speaks to the people of Ephesus, and lets them know he will probably never see them again, and that he knows he has done what he was called to do. He taught them about the life of Christ, and the salvation that is also theirs, through Jesus Christ. He will not be leaving them, and regretting that he did not do enough. Do you take the opportunity to speak of eternal salvation, when it has not come up, or do you wait for someone else to bring it up? Will you go to your final resting place with regrets of not talking to your best friends, and your family members about what Jesus did for each of us? Do you find it easier to speak to total strangers, because they don't know you and you don't care what they think of you? Go with confidence, to love and serve the Lord!

Lord, may I be an instrument of Your peace. May I love and serve You with my whole being, and live with no regrets.

Acts 20:17-27

May 20, 2015

Are you the type of person that people hate to see leave, or are you the type, people don't want to be around? Do you bring a sense of joy and happiness, so that people want to see you and talk to you, or do people know you are coming, so they find a way to get away? We have the choice every time we speak to someone, to make the experience a positive enlightening experience, or make it the visit they wish never happened. When Paul left Ephesus, the people wept, because they enjoyed his company, and what he said to them. He preached God's word to them, and they didn't want him to leave. He spoke with compassion and conviction, and they wanted to hear more. He spoke life giving words, and they couldn't get enough. Do you have the words people want to hear more of, or do you get chased away. It's part of you, you just need to find it, and start sharing it. Will you make someone smile today, and bring them life?

Lord, You alone have the words of everlasting life. May I be so bold as to deliver them in a way that people want to hear, and ask to hear more?

Acts 20:28-38

May 21, 2015

How do you react when you are being persecuted? When someone accuses you of something, that you know is not right, do you back down, or do you stand up and defend yourself? No matter how hard we try, not everyone is going to agree with us, or even want to see us do well. We sometimes feel it is a constant battle, and sometimes we just feel like giving in, because it's easier. But if, you know you're right, do you keep standing up, and taking the shots, or do you back away and give up? Paul recognized the crowd that he was speaking to, and some were taught the same as him, so he gained their trust by confirming what he believed, and knew they were also taught. He brought them to his side, so he did not have to fight this fight alone. Then he hears from the Lord, and knows that he still has work to do, so he will survive this trial. Will you withstand the trial, and go on to more, or will you back down, because it is easier?

Lord, may I always know You will give me the words to say, and the courage to stand before those who persecute me, that I may accomplish all You have asked me to be.

Acts 22:30; 23:6-11

May 22, 2015

Do you love me more than these? What do you own, that you truly feel you can't be without? What would happen if they were taken away from you? Do you so desire it, that if it was taken away, you would have to go get another one, a newer one, or more of it? Why do we get so attached to things that can be broken, or taken away? There's a certain part of us that wants, and sometimes, feels like needs. Jesus asks Peter a very pointed question, three times, after His resurrection. Was this to confront him on denying Jesus three times? Was it to challenge him, on what love really is? God wants us to love, but He also wants us to know what love is. It is a burning desire to be satisfied, and to feel need, and be fulfilled by that need. Our worldly things do not completely satisfy, they only provide temporary satisfaction. Think about the last thing you had to have. Do you now want a newer, or better one, or even more of it. God's love provides that complete satisfaction. Does that love make you want to feed His sheep? Is it so much that you want other people to feel that love?

Lord, You know that I love You. May I always desire to feed Your sheep, so that others will know Your love.

John 21:15-19

May 23, 2015

Are you concerned about the fate of other people? Why do some die young, or violently, and some seem to live a long life? Did the person that gets a long life do something right, and the others do something wrong, in God's eyes? Why do we torment ourselves over these questions? Why do we want to know everything? Isn't that how God created us? He gave us the ability to think, and to do things that some think, are not humanly possible. He even gave us the ability to think about whether God exists or not. Does He want us to understand the things that don't make sense? Why was John the only disciple that was not martyred, and all the rest died a violent death, for what they believed, and taught? Didn't John also preach Jesus' resurrection life also? John was imprisoned on an island and died, apparently of natural causes, old age. He is attributed to writing the book of Revelation. He is also the Apostle that is said to be the one that Jesus loved. Was there some reason he did not die a martyrs death? Do you question God for things you don't understand? Do you pray about them?

Lord, we have all seen, or heard about things that question You, may we see the love that You have for us, and know that is enough.

John 21:20-25

May 24, 2015

Do you know the power of the Holy Spirit? Do you know the gifts of the Holy Spirit? In the Catholic Church, and some other main line churches, we celebrate Pentecost 40 days after Easter. It is when Jesus handed on to the Apostles His gift to them, to go do as God had called them to do. This is also where Jesus handed on the command for Apostles, and those that they pass it on to, to forgive sins (confession). It is very likely you will see a lot of people wearing red today, as it is the color associated with the Holy Spirit, and the color that is associated with this day. Isaiah foretold the seven-fold gifts that the Spirit would give: wisdom, understanding, counsel, fortitude, knowledge, piety, and fear of the Lord (Isaiah 11:2). Do you ask to be strengthened by the Holy Spirit? Do you recognize these gifts in yourself? Which of them do you ask to receive more of?

Lord, may I know Your Spirit, and be strengthened by it, that I may know You more deeply, and love others as You love me.

John 20: 19-23

May 25, 2015

If you have a lot of money, can you still get to Heaven? Where are your riches? Do you help others with the money you have, or do you consider it all yours, because you earned it? Does that mean that a poor man, will automatically make it to Heaven? The man with many possessions came to Jesus asking what he must do to get to Heaven, knowing that he had followed all the commandments. Did he forget the most important commandments, to love God above all, and to have no other gods before Him? If we are obsessed with our money and our possessions to the point of forgetting about our fellow man, and not thanking God for all that we have, are we then worshipping those possessions more than God? How hard is it focus on God, when we are consumed with trying to make ourselves happy with money and material things? Is there something wrong with being driven to succeed? What is the end goal? Do you serve God, or what you own? Sometimes success is seen by what we own, but does that really make you happy, or just temporarily satisfied?

Lord You know my heart better than I know it myself, may I know You and love You more than the things I own.

Mark 10:17-27

May 26, 2015

Do you serve the Lord, and give alms, or tithe? Do you do it for God, or for yourself? There is a fine line when you serve. We do it for God, but sometimes we get in the way, we want to see or hear the praise, from others, to acknowledge we are doing good. I have been teaching Catechism for about 25 years, from fifth grade through Confirmation, and you appreciate when someone says something nice to you about what you do. You try not to let it go to your head, as if it was because of you. I didn't learn this overnight. It takes a lot of time and effort, but I do it for the Lord, and the people that are touched, are touched by God through the work He has called me to do. All glory be to God for the gifts He has given me, and the courage to be who I am. There are no regrets in the work that I do, but some will ask, "What good are you doing?" My response is, "it is not mine to know, I do it all for His Glory". Can I really make a difference? Can you make a difference? Do you feel you owe it to the Lord, for all that He has blessed you with? Where can you make a difference?

Lord, I know You and love You, and You give me reason to carry on, not that I owe You, but that I want to serve You.

Sirach 35:1-12

May 27, 2015

Isn't competition great? What are we competing for? Are we trying to be the best at something, or are we just wanting to be recognized for who we are, or what other people think of us? We all have a certain competitiveness in something, whether it is sports, grades, work, or even money. Who is it for? Ourselves, or someone else? When we were younger, we always fought over who would get to sit in the front seat by the door, when we went somewhere in the car. If we knew it early enough, we would say it so everyone knew we got "front seat by the door". Seems kind of silly now, but back then, we just wanted to be the first to say it. Now we want the best position at our job, or the best house, or the best car, or even a family that doesn't embarrass you. Jesus had to deal with that, even in his time. James and John wanted to sit at Jesus' right and His left. They wanted the place of honor, without knowing what it entailed, because they would look good to, "who?" God? We forget that we serve people, and therefore God by what we do. He would put us in a place of honor, if we deserved it, we don't have to call it. How hard is it to live as a servant, instead of trying to be the best at something only people see? Doesn't that depend on what you are trying to be the best at? Are you seen by God, and by others for what you do? Does it glorify God, or you?

God, may I live a life of servitude, that You may be glorified by my actions, not me by Yours.

Mark 10:32-45

May 28, 2015

How badly do you want to know the truth? Do you really want to see? Would you call out in a crowd of people to let them know you want to know the truth? Bartimaeus had never been able to see, and knew that Jesus was performing miracles, and could help him see, but how badly did he want to see? Will he make it known to all the people around him that he can't see? Our spiritual life is like that of Bartimaeus'. We want to know the truth but we're not sure we want others to know that we want it. If God did not create the world/universe, how did it come to be? Could it be from a big bang? How can something start from nothing? Didn't something have to provide the elements that started the big bang? Wouldn't that have to be God? What if there were no Heaven, or no hell? What would our purpose be? Would it be for the good of the human race? What's the purpose if it's just reincarnation, and we just come back as something better or worse, depending on our previous life, if we don't remember our previous life? What's the best thing we can come back as, if we live the perfect life? Wouldn't it be humans? Aren't we created in God's perfect image already? Wouldn't Heaven be the best thing to happen, if we had to live a perfect life, to get somewhere? Wouldn't God know it is nearly impossible for us to live a perfect life? Wouldn't He want us to be with Him? Why not send His Son Jesus to show us the way to Heaven? Why would Bartimaeus not want us to be able to see? Why are we afraid to ask, and let other people know that we want this? Will you have the courage to stand before people you have known for a long time, and ask for God to let you see? Will you accept it when He does let you see?

Lord, thank You for the gift of spiritual vision and the gift of sight, may I use them both for your glory.

Mark 10:46-52

May 29, 2015

What about the fig tree? Why did the fig tree get cursed, and wither to its roots? Is this some sort of distraction? It was not the season for figs, and it didn't have fruit on it, so Jesus curses it, and it withered and died. Why? Jesus then teaches us to pray, and believe that God will answer our prayers, we only need to believe that He will answer our prayers. Is there something about being always ready, no matter the time? Then there is this alleluia verse based on John 15:16: "I chose you from the world,/ to go and bear fruit that will last, says the Lord." Are these readings supposed to go together? We don't always get what we want when we ask God, but do we believe? Do we truly believe? If we do, does that belief last? We have to persevere, even when it isn't our time. How hard is it to believe, and trust, when we don't understand why? Do you ask God? Do you listen? After reading about the fig tree, I stressed about it and prayed about it, and here I am, going, what about the fig tree? Maybe there are things we are just not supposed to understand right now, maybe that's why we have to hang on to that last fruit, for someone who desperately needs it. Are you holding out for someone, or some situation that you just don't understand, why nothing is changing from your prayer? Do you believe? Truly trust that God will answer your prayer. I'm still praying about the fig tree.

Lord, I know there are things we may never know, or understand in this life time, but may I always trust that You know best, and that I stay always faithful to Your call.

Mark 11:11-26

May 30, 2015

Do you pray for wisdom? Do you want to know the truth, or do you want someone, or something to confirm what you already believe? The religious authorities wanted Jesus to tell them if He was the Messiah they so desperately sought, or if He was from man. They already knew what they wanted to believe, but they wanted it to come from the source of their problem. In today's reading from the Old Testament, we have (Sirach 51:12-20) a prayer for wisdom. Don't we all want wisdom? Knowing what is the ultimate truth? Isn't that something we all seek? But, what if it doesn't line up with what you have come to believe? What if it is completely opposite of what you believe to be truth? What if there is a spiritual battle for the truth that we seek? This is the kind of thing, a lot of people don't like to acknowledge. They want it clean and simple. They don't want to hear about anything that can be perceived as coming from evil, when they think about God. They don't want to acknowledge that there is evil in the world, working against the forces of God. Some of you seek answers, and message me, and email me, seeking the answers you so desperately want, and need. I appreciate that you trust I know, and I welcome your messages. These reflections cause me to pray, A LOT. Because I ask questions, I get more questions. I am not the most capable person to answer, but I also seek the wisdom, that is from God. Will you pray for wisdom? Do you want to know the truth?

Lord, You are the truth, and the wisdom that makes me stronger. May I always trust You're with me, and be strengthened by it.

Mark 11:27-33

May 31, 2015

How hard is it for you to go and make disciples of all nations? There are not a lot of people willing to go out and be a presence of the Holy Trinity to the world. Jesus did not say, go out and live your life, as if I came here for no reason, He said "All power in heaven and on earth has been given to me. Go, therefore, and make disciples of all nations, baptizing them in the name of the Father, and of the Son, and of the Holy Spirit, teaching them to observe all that I have commanded you. And behold, I am with you always, until the end of the age."(Matthew 28:19-20) He wants us to baptize in the name of the Holy Trinity. He wants us to immerse the people in His love, and His Father's lover, and the love of the Holy Spirit. As Catholics, we here the priest say this at the end of every Mass, as a command to go to love and serve the Lord. Do you go and do as we are commanded? Do you fear persecution? Isn't the Holy Spirit with you, as well as me?

My God and my Father, may I go and make believers of Your undying love, and that I will fear no evil, because you are with me always.

Romans 8:14-17

Matt 28:16-20

June 1, 2015

Do you know what a cornerstone is? It is the part of the foundation that the whole house or building is built around. If it is not in place, the whole building is out of place. It is the base of the foundation. As Christians we see Christ as the base of all that we hold to be truth. He has taught us through His words and His actions how God wants us to live. God has given us the ability to care for His people, and help them to understand what He wants for us, yet we want it our way, and not God's way, so we fail at keeping our cornerstone in place. It seems too simple to say follow Jesus' example, when we look at the world as a place we can do our own thing, and not feel that we have to be held responsible for our actions. If you were responsible for someone else's things, would you take care of them like they were yours? When you are told to be accountable, do you turn and walk away? What do you hold as your cornerstone, or truth?

Lord, You are the cornerstone of all that I hold to be truth, may I always trust that You stay firm and do not change.

Mark 12:1-12

June 2, 2015

Have you ever had to prove something to a group or an individual? Why do we so easily fall apart when someone challenges us on what we feel we know to be true? What part did the coin play in this questioning? They had one ready when Jesus asked for it. Did they anticipate Jesus asking for the coin? All ruling bodies had their own money, and it usually had the image of the leader at the time the money was circulating. The answer seems simple now, that you should give to Caesar what is Caesar's, but what if you were asked the same question? Should you pay all your taxes? Do you fudge numbers on your taxes, so you don't have to pay as much? Because we are still part of the world, we still have to obey worldly laws. But, do you give to God what is God's? What is God's portion? Is it a set price, or is it what you feel right with?

Lord, may I not feel that I am indebted to You, but do everything in my power to acknowledge You as the reason for my being.

Mark 12:13-17

June 3, 2015

Have you ever really thought about what happens after the death of your human body? Today's reading, the Sadducees confront Jesus to argue their point that there is no resurrection after death. They didn't believe in resurrection, that's why they're "sad u see". Do you still maintain your spouse in the afterlife? That is their question. Do we become angels, as some people say, when someone dies? Aren't angels all spiritual, and of God? Aren't we human, with a spirit? It doesn't seem possible that we could become angels. Don't we resurrect with our new bodies? Then again, God can do anything can't He? I think of an old movie that was out about 30 years ago called "Cocoon". The Old people were given the opportunity to live forever, in a spirit form, and not on earth as human anymore. They were all in, except one, who wanted to stay in the human life. We sometimes grow so attached to this life, that we don't want to let go, and trust that what is in store for us is far better, than what is here. Will you see your loved ones in Heaven? Are you doing everything in your power to help them, and yourself, end up there?

Lord Your mysteries are only mysteries to us, as we do not know all the answers, but You have given me reason to trust in You, and know that there are reasons we do not understand everything.

Mark 12:18-27

June 3, 2015

This is the second one for the day. This gospel reading is not from the daily readings of the Catholic Lectionary daily readings, it is by request from a friend.

Which is harder to deal with, the loss, or the fear of loss? So many times, in this time of modern medicine, we hear someone is dying, well before they die. Sometimes knowing someone is dying is harder on us because we are not sure how to act around that person, or what we should say, because it could be the last we see them. Both of my parents succumbed to cancer, and both knew about how long they had to live. I remember being with my family in their last hours, to say goodbye, and not knowing what would be the last word we would hear from them. Would it leave a lasting impression? Would it mean anything? What do you do with the person you know may not be around very long? Do you make every moment a memory, or do you just go on living, and be the memory? Why do we fear loss so much? Don't we already have the memories with them? Do you have time to make more with them? When was the last time you listened to the song, "Cats in the cradle"?

Lord You give us so many chances to make memories, may I always remember that when I am with someone.

John 11: 35-44

June 4, 2015

Do you know all Ten Commandments? If you know the two great commandments, all ten are encompassed in these two. We think of this as easy because we should be able to love God with all we are, but there are so many things that get in our way. How many of you have read one of these reflections, or another daily devotion, and a couple feeds later in Facebook, you caught yourself going against what you just were inspired by. We are a very easily distracted kind of people. What about loving your neighbor as yourself? That too sounds very easy, but not everybody loves themselves, in a healthy way. If you think about doing to others as you would have done unto you, then you are a little closer to loving your neighbor. When someone does wrong by you, can you take 20 seconds, or longer if you like, to pray for that person, or the situation? What helps me, is thinking about that person as a child, and wondering how they came to be who they are. We don't always know their situation, and that is not an excuse, but sometimes taking yourself away from the situation can give you a better vision of what just happened. Will you take time to pray for those who persecute you? Can it hurt? Only if we let it.

Lord, I ask that Your love guide me through the times I do not understand, and may Your love help me see as You see.

Mark 12:28-34

June 5, 2015

How hard is it for you to claim Jesus Christ is Lord? Do you want Him to reign over your life? Do you want anyone to set the rules that you live by? By nature, we as humans say we want control of our lives, but then we still want someone to set the rules, and enforce them. Why is that? Is it so we have reason to show someone else what they have done wrong? Is it so everyone plays by the same rules? What if the other people don't live by the same rules you live by. It is hard to convince someone that God is God of all, and that Jesus Christ is our Lord, when the only thing you can use is the Bible. Not everyone believes the Bible to be their source of the truth. How do you convince someone of God's love for us, without using the Bible? Is your life, and the lives of other people that proclaim Jesus Christ as Lord, an example of God's love? If not, how are you going to convince the person that thinks the Bible is just something written by a bunch of different people, striving to make people believe the way they believe? To some people, the Bible is just another book. Does your life proclaim Jesus Christ as Lord? If not, what do you need to change?

Jesus Christ, my Lord, and my God, may I live my life to reflect the love You have for me, and all Your people. May You be glorified in what I say, and what I do.

Mark 12:35-37

June 6, 2015

Let me first say, Thank you to all who read these!

What is your life like? Do you have times when you feel like God has left you behind, does not care about you? This reading from Tobit is wrapping up the readings from the week. If you have time, read that book in the Bible, it is our daily lives and how we deal with them. I will give the "Readers Digest" version. Tobit fell on hard times, but he continued to do God's will, and bury the dead, even when people tried to kill him for it. He continued to pray for God's intervention. Tobiah, his son, was at the age to marry, and Sarah, a cousin, had tried seven times to marry, and never made it to consummate the marriage. So Tobiah was sent to marry Sarah, and before they went to bed he and Sarah prayed. The Angel Raphael was with them and even returned to the home of Tobit with them. So they had hardships in their life, and they didn't give up on God, they prayed for God to be with them. They thanked God for all they had, and didn't ask God why He forgot about them. How do you handle the trials of this life? Do you give up, or do you trust that God knows more than you, and He will provide?

Lord may I always trust in You and know that You will never leave me to go it alone.

Tobit 12:1, 5-15, 20

June 7, 2015

Are you Catholic, and do you believe in the true presence of Jesus Christ in the Holy Eucharist? As Catholics we believe that the bread and wine that we share at each Mass is consecrated into Jesus' body and blood. The last supper that we see in the Gospels, has Jesus telling the disciples, "Take it; this is my body." Then he took a cup, gave thanks, and gave it to them, and they all drank from it. He said to them, "This is my blood of the covenant, which will be shed for many." We also see in John chapter 6, Jesus explaining to the disciples, after He feeds the 5,000, that He is true bread that came down from Heaven, and His body is the bread, and His blood is the drink, and whoever eats His body will have everlasting life. This so distressed some of the followers, that they left Jesus, and Jesus didn't call them back to tell them, He was only speaking symbolically, He let them leave. This is a hard teaching for some, and requires prayer, to help you understand, but the Catholic Church teaches that this transubstantiation happens during the Mass, and that we receive Jesus each time we receive communion during Mass. Today is the Solemnity of the most Holy Body and Blood of Christ. Is this teaching too hard to believe? You will find that not every Catholic really understands this teaching, as I'm sure some of you that are not Catholic will believe it. I only ask that you prayerfully read John Chapter 6 to see why the Catholic Church teaches the true presence of Christ in the Eucharist.

Lord God, You gave Your Son for us to know You and understand You better, but sometimes the teachings are hard. May Your Holy Spirit guide me, and help me know You more completely.

Mark 14:12-16, 22-26

June 8, 2015

What does it mean to be without something? Do we struggle with it because we have it, or is it harder to understand when you have never really had it? The Beatitudes are hard to understand when you read them without doing it prayerfully, because we don't understand how you can be poor in spirit and have the Kingdom of Heaven, or meek and inherit the land. Does it mean that because you are without, so you will appreciate it more when you receive it? When you dig a little deeper, you see that we are being taught what it's like to be rich in spirit. The merciful will be shown mercy, those who hunger and thirst will be satisfied, the clean of heart will see God, and the peacemakers will be called children of God. We need to want for the right things, not the material things that the people around us approve of, but what God knows we need to be clean of heart. How hard is it for you to be humble? People that know me well, know that is not necessarily one of my character traits, so it is not always easy. If you are struggling through tough times, do you think of God, or are you mad at Him, because of the trials? Were the prophets and the disciples of Jesus tried, and persecuted?

Lord I know You do not chase away Your faithful through persecution, but many times Your faithful will leave You because of the trials they face, may You show them You are with them.

Matt 5:1-12

June 9, 2015

So, if you never tasted salt, what would it be to you? Doesn't it look like some sort of stone, or sand? What if you never told anyone about your faith in God, and in Jesus Christ, and who the Holy Spirit is to you? Wouldn't you look just like anyone else walking on this earth? How would anyone know you are Christian, if they never really experienced you, as a Christian? Does your light shine so that others can see that you are a Christian by what you do? This lesson from Matthew's Gospel is a strong argument for evangelizing. There aren't too many people that are willing to go out to the people, and show them what it is like to be Christian. Are you willing to be the salt and light that Jesus calls all His disciples to be? What about the light that shines within you? Wouldn't you allow someone to see the light in the darkness that they live in, if you knew it would give them hope and life? Go! Be the light, and the salt that provides the hope of Jesus Christ!

Lord, may I show people the way to You, through the love that You and others, have shared with me.

Matt 5:13-16

June 10, 2015

Do you pay attention, when there are little kids around? Do you watch them learn from the people that are around them? They're like little sponges, taking in everything. They hear what we say. They see what we do. They see how we act in certain situations. Do you ever see them do something, and wonder where they learned that, or hear them say a swear word for the first time, and wonder where they heard it? They don't have to be staring at you, to learn what you are doing, they just grab it, and absorb it. What about the things you do, that you think are just little lies? We teach them not to lie, but we catch them lying. We do something like, keep the extra change when the cashier gives us too much change, for what we gave them. Those little eyes catch that, and they don't differentiate that from stealing, the way some people would. It is stealing, and lying, but they saw a parent do it, so now it is all okay. How easy is it for you to lead a child astray, by what you do and what you say? Be careful little eyes, what you see.

How I love your law, Lord!/ I study it all day long. (Psalm 119:97)

Matt 5:17-19

June 11, 2015

Are you holding a grudge, or contentment for anyone? How hard is it for you to forgive, or even ask for forgiveness? I don't think very many of us are able to completely release the bad feelings, or hurt we have for someone who has wronged us. When you hang on to it, does it make you feel better? It seems like we let it fester and get under us, to the point that we are the one that seems like we're being punished for something someone else did? Is this a sort of punishment for the lack of forgiveness? We need to learn forgiveness for our own good. How many times have you felt contentment for someone for so long, it was making you crazy, and when you finally approached the person about it, they didn't even remember it? They let it go, yet you were still being tormented by it. Who is your brother? Isn't that any of God's children, not just our blood relatives? Doesn't that mean we need to make things right with everyone? Will you take the time to contact that one person that is holding you from the Kingdom of Heaven?

Lord, I lift up to You all those who need Your strength to go to those that need to seek forgiveness from someone, or need to give forgiveness.

Matt 5:20-26

June 12, 2015

What does it mean to pour your life out for someone? Have you ever done, what seems like, everything you can for someone, and they didn't appreciate it? There are people that, it seems, you just cannot impress. They don't acknowledge what you have done for them. There are many people that are very hard to impress. This reading from the Gospel of John, tells about Jesus being pierced while He is still on the cross, and blood and water flowed from Him. Is there symbolism there? Is the blood a representation of the Eucharist (the body and blood of Christ), and the water a representation of Baptism? Is that what Jesus did when He poured his life out for us? Yet some people do not appreciate what He did. They don't acknowledge how much He poured Himself out for you and me. How hard is it to see what He did, and appreciate it? Have you shared that with the people that are closest to you?

Lord, Thank You for everything, and especially the blood that You poured out, so that we may have everlasting life.

John 19:31-37

June 13, 2015

How hard is it for you to always tell the truth? As I have aged, it seems it is hard for me, not to tell the truth. However, that is not true for all people. There are people I know, that will say whatever they have to, to make themselves look better to those in leadership. But, isn't that kind of contradictory? If you always are truthful, you never have to think about a story you've told, it is always what you did. If you lie about something, the story changes, because you have to think about the first story you told. How many times have you watched a movie, or show, and one of the characters started with a simple lie that seemed harmless, but as the show progressed, the lie made things worse? Those shows drive me crazy, because the truth would have had far fewer consequences than the little lie they started with. The Gospel reading today, Jesus talks about truth. Let your yes mean yes, and your no mean no. How much nicer is it to be around people that are always honest and truthful? Doesn't that allow you to trust them in all things, when you don't have to worry about the little things? Does your yes mean yes? Are you the person people can always trust?

Lord, the closer I have come to You the easier I find it to be always truthful and honest. May You be my guide, and my counsel.

Matt 5:33-37

June 14, 2015

What gives you the courage and strength to let people know about what it means to be Christian, and what Christ has done to grow your life into something beautiful? Have you ever thought about what impact Jesus made on the world? He was one man, and He took twelve nobodies, and as of right now there are approximately 2.2 billion Christians in the world. That is about 35% of the world population. In the Americas, we make up about 86% of the population. Is there still people that need to hear the word of Christ? Think about people that are near you, family, friends, co-workers, and strangers. Could you make a difference in their lives? Jesus was one man, albeit, God is present from birth in Him, but the 12 disciples were no different than you and I. One tiny seed grew into 2.2 billion people, (so you aren't alone in this). This is the kind of growth Jesus is speaking about in this parable. Did the disciples completely understand it, and think it was possible? Probably not. This is the same in you, and those you speak to, sometimes it only takes planting that one little seed in someone, and God takes over, and makes them into a massive tree, feeding many with His word. Can the Holy Spirit work in you as He did in the disciples? Will you let it happen, or will you suppress it from growth?

Holy Spirit, continue to grow in me, that I may go to the world, and continue to grow Your disciples, that You may be glorified.

Mark 4:26-34

June 15, 2015

What do you use to guide you, when someone confronts you, and you know it could get out of hand? I happen to be raised in a family that was taught to fight, to defend yourself, so when someone tells me turn the other cheek, I am not real receptive to it. Is it easy for you to not argue a point, or get defensive when someone attacks you? This is one of the hardest of Jesus' teachings for me. Did you know this is actually an Old Testament teaching? Let him give his cheek to the smiter, and be filled with insults (Lamentations 3:30). Most people will see an eye for an eye and a tooth for a tooth, and assume that means we are supposed to "get even", but even the teachings before Jesus did not teach that way. Why have we gotten to this? Is it the way we were created or is it the way we are brought up? There are a lot of people that don't believe in God that want world peace, and there are a lot of people that believe in God, that are OK with defense and war. Even if you don't believe in God, you were still created by God, but have made the choice to not believe in Him, by your God given gift. Why do the violent, God fearing people, get so much more attention? How will you handle it when someone offends you? Will you turn the other cheek, or lash out?

Lord, You know me, and know this is where I am weak. Help me to be more like You and less like me.

Matt 5:38-42

June 16, 2015

Are you perfect? Do you think you will ever become perfect? Jesus tells the disciples that we all need to become perfect, as the Father is perfect (Matthew 5:48). In the original Aramaic text the word was completeness, or wholeness, and our closest word was perfect. How do we get there? I'm sure we all have someone we don't like, or people that don't like us. Didn't God create us all? Aren't we all children of God? Some have chosen to acknowledge that, and some will deny it, but can they change that fact by not believing? Did you always believe? Do you think people were praying for you in those times when you were in your rebellious stage, or if you are still in it? It is easy to pray for those we don't like, or are persecuting us, when we remember that they are also children of God. Maybe that's where we need to be. Maybe completeness means being able to care for everybody, because they are all God's children. Wouldn't a parent want all their children to love each other, no matter what? The Holy Spirit helps us to become perfect, but we don't always listen. Will you allow the Holy Spirit to help you become perfect?

Holy Spirit guide me and help me to see even my enemies as God's children, so I can show the same compassion as our loving Father.

Mt 5:43-48

165

June 17, 2015

How hard is it for you to give to God, and those in need, when you don't have much for yourself? Have you ever been in a situation when you really didn't have much, and sometimes wondered where your next meal was coming from? When we were newly married, we didn't have much, a $200 wonder car, wondered how it still ran, and lived in an apartment for about $250 per month, along with a job that paid about $5/hour. Then Marie was born with heart problems. Any extra money was gone from visiting her in the cities, and the doctor bills. We still made it. Sometimes you make it through the tough times and you are stronger because of it. The only thing we were giving to God at that time was prayer. He took it, and got us through those times. We give where we can, because we know God will not forget about us, so we should always remember Him. Do you give, knowing that you can never out give God? Even when we moved for a year, we still owned our house in Cumberland and had a hard time making it, but we had people stop, out of nowhere and give us food. That is when we started teaching Catechism, because it was a way to give when we had no money. Do you give all you can, or just what you think you can afford? God does not let you down, and will always give you more then you give. Where will He bring you to? Do you trust in Him?

Lord, may I always know You are with me, and will never forget me.

2 Corinthians 9:6-11

June 18, 2015

How often do you pray? What do you pray for? Do you pray for help, when you are struggling? Do you pray to praise God for all He does, and who He is? Do you ask for the things of this world to be better, or are you waiting on Heaven? Do you ask for God to provide you what you need? Do you ask for forgiveness, and to be forgiven the way you forgive others? Do you ask to be saved from the evil of this world? These are all part of the Lord's Prayer. Sometimes when I'm at a loss for words, I say this prayer, to help me remember how Jesus taught us to pray. Do you remember who taught you to pray? Was it a family member? Was it a priest, or pastor? Was it a friend? Take time today, and say this prayer slowly, and let the words become the prayer of your every day. Pray for the person that taught you to pray, so that God's blessings may be with them.

Lord, I'm not sure who taught me to pray, but my earliest memory was of grandma making us say your prayer before we went to bed at night, when we stayed with her. May her soul be in Your loving presence.

Matt 6:7-15

June 19, 2015

How do you see the world? What do you watch? Have you wondered if you would be watching the same thing, if you had a 5 year old watching it with you? They ask a lot of questions, sometimes questions you really don't want to answer. They see things as they are, not as, just a show, as we sometimes try to convince ourselves. We see things in this world that can be pure evil, and sometimes we try to justify it, because we think it doesn't affect us. Do you see as God sees, or do you see as you have conditioned your brain to see? Most of us can push away the evil, as just that, and walk away from it, but there are people that see things differently, and they act out what they see, and try to imitate it, whether it's evil or not. We can all probably think about things we have seen, that we wish we could wash away, but sometimes our brain stores it some place that surfaces when we least expect it, and we have to revisit it. How hard is it for you to turn away, or turn off, something that you know is not good for your soul? Do you know your body is the temple of the Holy Spirit? Do you acknowledge that when something is on, that probably isn't good for you? How do you see the world, is it evil, and bad, or do you see that good that is also present?

> Lord, Give me your eyes for just one second
> Give me your eyes so I can see,
> Everything that I keep missing,
> Give your love for humanity.
> Give me your arms for the broken-hearted
> The ones that are far beyond my reach.
> Give me Your heart for the ones forgotten.
> Give me Your eyes so I can see.
> (Brandon Heath, "Give me Your Eyes")

Matt 6:19-23

June 20, 2015

How hard is it for you to not worry about money, or food, or material things? This teaching from Jesus to the disciples seems so simple, yet we all have a hard time not worrying. We worry about whether we have enough food, yet all animals find the food they need to sustain themselves. They have to work for it, but it is there. I have a good friend that says, "it's fly crap in pepper". Think about that. We could worry about it, but how would you even know if it's there? You can't see it, and you can't taste it, so why worry about it? What is more important to you, serving God, and loving Him, or whether you have nice clothes, nice car, or a nice house? What do those get you? Maybe someone is impressed with it, but what does it get you? It is an endless cycle, and never stops. Do you worry that God has forgotten about you? Did you wake up this morning? Did you remember Him, and thank Him for another day? It's the simple things in life that get us through, not what we have, and what other people think about us. Take the time today to thank Him for what you have, no matter how little you think it is.

Lord I thank You for my family, and providing me a job, and providing me food on the table. May I be ever mindful of all that You have provided me.

Matt 6:24-34

June 21, 2015

Have you had to endure storms, and trials in your life? Are you going through tough times now? Do you keep God with you at all times, and are you confident He will pull you through? Do you let Him take the wheel of your life, and have faith that He is always with you, and will protect you? Just because you put your faith in Jesus Christ, doesn't mean you are not going to go through some rough times. Jesus wasn't spared the trials, what makes us think we should have clear sailing? In this reading from Mark's Gospel, Jesus leads the disciples to the boat, and goes to rest, and when the storm comes the disciples panic and wake Jesus to let them know they are scared, and think they will die. Jesus was with them, and was leading them, and the storms came, and they didn't feel they could get through that storm, so they called on Jesus, and He calmed the storm. Did they lack faith, or did they just know where to go, in troubled times? Do you trust that God is with you, and will get you through? Do you have the faith to call on Jesus, when you don't think you can handle it anymore? Do you trust in Him to know He will bring you through?

Jesus, You have had the controls of my life, and many times I thought You left me on my own, but when I called on You, You carried me through. May I be ever mindful of Your presence in my life, and always have faith in You.

Mark 4:35-41

June 22, 2015

How easy is it for you to have preconceived ideas of what someone believes, without knowing what they truly believe? Because I am more open about who God is, and what Jesus Christ has done for me, people don't think of me as a Catholic Christian. I'm sure a lot of that stems from what they were taught, or what they have seen. There are a lot of misunderstandings of who we are, and some Catholics aren't as open about their faith as I am, to explain what we believe. I have had people tell me, before they know I'm Catholic, that Catholics have it all wrong, and do things that are not biblical. When they are pressed into explaining what they mean, they usually tell me something that they heard or read somewhere that was not Catholic teaching. Why would we, as Christians, criticize other Christians about what we believe? Wouldn't we be better served to teach people about Jesus Christ and what He did for you, and for me? Isn't that what Jesus taught? We look so hard at each other to find fault in their ways, that we forget what we are trying to accomplish. We don't need to get other Christians to believe what we believe, we need to help unbelievers understand who Jesus is, and what He has done for us. We don't need to condemn, we only need to show them what God has done, and can do for all who believe. Can you look at people, and not judge, or is that the only way you see? Do you need to look deeper into yourself, before you look at someone else?

Lord, may I see without judgement, and remember that is about You and not about me.

Matthew 7:1-5

June 23, 2015

How do you know when something is right? Do you take the easy path, or the one less traveled? Our human nature would have us take the easy way, the one that causes the least amount of stress. We don't look for the narrow gate in life, we always want the one that is easier to get through. If you've ever been to a concert, or sporting event, you know that everyone is trying to get in the large gate, and that line doesn't move very fast. If you could only enter where the performers, and athletes enter. How much easier would that be? If you choose to follow Jesus' teachings, and live as He has taught us, you can enter the same narrow gate into Heaven, but that isn't always the easy way. If you let the Holy Spirit guide your way, it is easy. We just don't like to be told where to go, and what to do, so we don't always follow His guidance. Will you listen when the Holy Spirit guides you to the narrow gate, or will you follow the large crowds?

Lord, Your Holy Spirit has shown me ways I have not been willing to follow in the past, because I wanted easy. May I know You are leading me to far greater things, and follow where you lead me.

Matt 7:6, 12-14

June 24, 2015

Did God form you in the womb? Did he create you for a purpose? Today we recognize St. John the Baptist, and all readings are attributed to Him. The prophet Isaiah prophesies about a man to be called from the womb, to go to the people, and announce the coming of the Messiah. John was destined to be born, and his life was to be for the soul purpose of announcing Jesus Christ as the Messiah. He died a tragic death, yet he fulfilled his purpose, to announce Jesus Christ. John knew his purpose from the womb. Some of us go through our whole life wondering what our purpose is. We wonder sometimes if we have come far enough and God has fulfilled His purpose for us. He definitely formed you in the womb, and He has a purpose for you, but have you sought Him out, and asked Him to help you know what it is? Do you want to know what it is? Would it scare you to know that it may not be what you want it to be? Will you pray for answers?

Lord I now know some of what you have planned for me, but this may only be the first step in where You are leading me. May I be willing to go where You lead me.

Isaiah 49:1-6

June 25, 2015

What happens when the storms of this life come crashing at you doors, and windows? Are you able to stand up to them, and face them with the confidence you will come through? Jesus tells of houses that are built on sand, and houses built on rock. Is your Faith like that of the house built on sand, that you do nothing to make it stronger, so when the storms come, you and your family come crashing down? Or, is your faith built on the rock that is Jesus Christ that makes you want to do more to become stronger, so when the storms come, you can withstand it? It's interesting that just before He speaks of where the houses are built, He says, "Not everyone who says to me, 'Lord, Lord,' will enter the Kingdom of heaven, but only the one who does the will of my Father in heaven"(Matthew 7:21). Is that saying that just because you say all the right things, that, will not get you to Heaven? Is Jesus saying that you need to do His will, or His work, in order to get to Heaven? Is that what helps us to have a rock solid foundation? Will you strengthen your foundation with prayer, and doing God's will? Will Jesus know you when you come before the Father, or will He say, "I never knew you. Depart from me you evildoer"(Matthew 7:23)?

Lord, may I always know what to do, and how to serve You. May I not fear the world before me, and be ever ready to do Your work, with a grateful heart for Your love.

Matthew 7:21-29

June 26, 2015

How do you react when you are approached by someone you are unfamiliar with? Do you turn and walk away, or do you stay and do whatever is needed? In today's reading, a leper approaches Jesus to be healed. In those days, a leper would be equivalent to someone approaching you with a knife, if you touched them, or they touched you, you were almost certainly going to die a slow and agonizing death. Jesus did what everyone should do for those that are hurting, or in distress. He touched the leper. He was not concerned whether He was going to die from leprosy, He touched the leper. How often do we see people in need, and we stay away, because we're afraid of getting too close. You see the violence in the world, and it makes you wonder, if someone would have taken the time to reach out to these people, would they have gotten to that point? Yes, some have been brainwashed, but what if someone saw their pain, and reached out to them, and showed they cared enough to touch them? The power of touch. Everyone is afraid they will catch some disease, so they have stopped touching each other. When you are talking to someone you care for, or you see someone in need of help, touch them, and show them you care. Sometimes that little touch, will open their soul. Do you bring your troubles to Jesus, and let Him touch your heart, and heal you?

Lord may Your healing power of touch be with me today, that I may reach the person that needs to feel human contact, to know You are there.

Matt 8:1-4

175

June 27, 2015

How far will you go when it could be the difference between life or death? The centurion was a Roman soldier, and was not supposed to be following, or even associating with people like Jesus, who were preaching God's word. He cared for his servant enough to risk possibly being criticized, or even losing his position, to approach this man, Jesus, who he had seen curing people. Do you risk what other people think of you, to approach Jesus, and ask for His help? Do you value position more than the life, or well-being of those you care for? Then we see Jesus cure Peter's mother-in-law. What did she do after she was healed? She immediately got up and started serving Jesus. Are you that grateful when God performs the miracles in your life? Do you immediately get up and start serving God? Do you recognize God, and ask Him to help you, even if other people do not accept that?

Lord, I am eternally grateful for all that you have done in my life. May I serve You with all that I am.

Matt 8:5-17

June 27, 2015

What do you use as a moral compass? How do you determine what is right and what is wrong? Is it determined by what certain people say is right? Are you alright with a man in his twenties marrying a woman in her twenties? How about a man in his fifties marrying a woman in her teens? What about a man marrying a man, or a woman marrying a woman? How about a woman in her thirties marrying a boy in his teens? What about a man in his thirties marrying a boy twelve years old? How about a woman in her forties wanting to marry a boy twelve? What if people said they want everybody to have the right to do whatever they want, and some man wanted an eight year old? When do you draw the line, and what do you use to make that determination? I think Christians are getting a bad rap here because they are using a moral compass that is what God tells them, in the Bible. Is that wrong to have a moral compass, to determine right from wrong? What do you use?

June 28, 2015

Did Jesus decide who would be healed and who would not be healed? Didn't He heal anybody, and everybody that came to Him for healing? He even left what He was doing, to help people in need. We sometimes focus so much on what we are doing, that we forget that there are people that can use our help. More importantly, we forget to tell people that need more healing than we can provide, that they can take it to God in prayer. If we truly believe He can heal, and He has helped us, why don't we tell people He can help them? Are we afraid they will think bad of us? The people were telling Jesus to go away, because there was nothing He could do anymore, because the girl was dead. They thought enough to send for Him when they thought He could heal her, but they didn't have the faith to believe He could bring someone back from the dead. Is your faith as strong as the woman with the hemorrhage that knew if she could just touch Jesus, she would be healed, or do you draw a line as to what is too much for God? Is there such a thing? Do you believe fully, or just a little?

My God and my Father, You can do all things, but as humans, we sometimes doubt that You are still in control, and sometimes we try to decide what You can, and cannot do. May I always know, there is never too much for You.

Mark 5:21-43

June 29, 2015

Has anyone ever challenged your faith, and challenged you personally for what you believe? How do you respond? Do you first wonder why they are testing you, and then wonder if you did something to make them question what you believe? Why did Jesus ask Peter, three times, "Do you love me? (John 21:15)" Didn't Peter deny Jesus three times on the night He was taken in to be crucified? Three times Jesus commands him to go to His people and tend to them, and feed them. Peter is a lot like you and I. He wants to be better, and he is always trying but he occasionally fails, and is held accountable for what he has done. He doesn't really understand what He has done that makes Jesus question him, but He always does what Jesus tells him to do. Peter was challenged, and was able to become one of the great apostles, and the first Pope. Jesus didn't do it to ridicule him, He did it to make him stronger. Today is the day a lot of churches recognize Peter and Paul, as the great leaders of our Christian faith. They became great, because they were challenged. Nothing great comes to us if we are not challenged to become more. Do you welcome challenges, or do fall apart because of them? What makes you stronger?

Lord, You have challenged me to be better, and there are times I back away, and sulk because of them, but You keep challenging me, not to make me weak, but to make me stronger. Thank You!

John 21:15-19

June 30, 2015

Have you ever felt like God was leading you away from something for your own good, but you struggled with letting go? How do you let go of the things you have become comfortable with, even when you know they are not necessarily good for you? Lot, the nephew of Abraham, had gone to Sodom with his family, and became accustomed to what was happening there. He may have known, or felt what was happening was wrong, but he, and his family chose to stay, and live in that city. Abraham had even pleaded to save the city if there were as few as ten righteous people living there, and God agreed, but Lot's house was the only ones saved. The reading just before this, shows the men of the town coming to seize the two Angels to have sexual relations with them, and were only stopped be the two Angels. If you have time, read Genesis chapters 18 & 19. As Lot and his family were leaving Sodom, Lot's wife could not resist looking back on the city, even though they were told not to. She could not let go of her past, and it destroyed her. Do you struggle with letting go of your past, even when you know deep down it is not good for you, even when you know God pulled you away from it, to save you? What keeps you from looking back? What pulls you back? The Holy Spirit can give you the strength you need to not look back, if only you seek His help.

Lord, You can do anything, and You can save me from my past errors, if only I trust You, and follow when You lead me.

Genesis 19:15-29

July 1, 2015

Do you have step children, or know someone with them? Why do we even call them step children? That may have something to do with why they seem to be treated differently, or is it because they are not our blood? Abraham had Ishmael with Sarah's maid servant, Hagar, with Sarah's approval, and after Sarah had Isaac, she didn't want to have Ishmael and Hagar stay around, because she was possessive of the inheritance from Abraham. You notice Abraham did not condemn Sarah for wanting this, he did what he had to, to make her happy, even if it meant never seeing Ishmael again. How many times do you witness this in families that you know, and it makes your heart break? What do you do to make it better? Can you do anything, without offending the parents? You can release it and let God handle it, or you can point it out. Are you willing to risk that for the child, even if it offends the parents? How do you handle those situations when you worry that it will have lasting effects on the child? What can you do?

Lord, may Your blessings be with those little ones, that have done nothing to be in that position, that you may open the eyes of the parents, and help them see, so the little ones will know Your love.

Gen. 21:5, 8-20a

July 2, 2015

Today's reading is long, but worth it.

Have you ever wondered why there are so many references to Abraham in the Old and New Testament of the Bible? This story is one that shocked me the first time I read it, and tells a lot about faith. If you had conversations with God, regularly, and He asked you to go to a mountain with your son, the one He had promised you for so long, and told you to offer him up as a sacrifice, would you do it? Isaac was wondering where the sacrifice was, and Abraham said, "God will provide"(Genesis22:8). Abraham showed a faith in God that very few have before Him, or since. Ultimately God provides the ram for sacrifice, and hints at the sacrifice He will do for our sins, when He sends His own Son, to die on the cross, as the last sacrifice needed. Do you have that kind of faith, to trust that God will always provide for you, if only you trust in Him, and know that He is in control?

Lord, Your examples of faith that You have shown us throughout the Bible, still shock me, when I should know that we can all have that kind of faith. Forgive me for not always trusting that I have nothing to worry about.

Genesis 22:1b-19

July 4, 2015

Why is the Bible comprised of the Old Testament and the New Testament? Isn't it all one? This reading we hear Jesus reference new and old wine skins. The stories of Jesus' life and resurrection are life changing and need to be in a new section. It does not wipe away the old, but brings it to deeper meaning and understanding of God's plan, and what the prophets were saying. When you read the Old Testament you see how the people tried to serve God and failed, because, like you and I, they sinned. They thought that their sins would not get them to Heaven, and they sinned all the more. We have Jesus in the New Testament forgiving our sins through His sacrificial death and resurrection, and He provides us the new hope of Heaven. Have you read both the New and Old Testament accounts of God's mercy, and the prophets pointing to Jesus?

Lord every time I read Your word, I am amazed at the new things You show me. May I be ever persistent in knowing You deeper, and loving You more.

Matt 9:14-17

July 5, 2015

Do you have something in your life that seems nearly impossible to rid yourself of? Is it something you feel completely powerless against? Do you feel weak because of it, or does it make you stronger? People that know me, and have seen me eat, know that I have a form of turrets, that causes me to completely stop in mid chew, and makes me take a lot longer to eat. I have asked God to please release this from me, but He has not. Sometimes I wonder why this burden will not leave, but I realize it may never be gone from me. This verse from 2 Corinthians gives me hope and strength, knowing that even the Apostle Paul had some sort of thorn in his life that caused him the same sort of distress. Sometimes these little "inconvenient" things in our lives do make us stronger. As Paul says, "Therefore, I am content with weaknesses, insults, hardships, persecutions, and constraints, for the sake of Christ; for when I am weak, then I am strong"(2 Corinthians 12:10). Do you look at your weakness as a strength, and know that God is in it? Do you let it beat you, or are you strengthened by it?

Lord, I don't understand why this thorn has been put into my life, but I will use it as a strength, not a weakness.

2 Corinthians 12:7-10

July 6, 2015

Have you ever put conditions on your faith in God? Sometimes we see the opportunity for God to make something better for us, or for someone we care for, and if He does do that good, we will remain faithful to God. This reading from the book of Genesis, is the scene when Jacob sees a stairway to Heaven. This is where the reference to "Jacob's ladder" comes from. Jacob is the son of Isaac, who stole the "first born" blessing from his brother Esau. Jacob puts a condition on God, that he will accept Him as his God, if He protects him on his journey. Why do we put conditions on God? Why do we feel that if God answers this prayer, or that request, our faith will be stronger? Is it the sign we are looking for to help us believe? Jacob had just seen the stairway to Heaven, and that didn't convince him! What are you waiting on to put your faith fully in God's hands? Are you still waiting for a sign, or is your faith sufficient?

Lord God, I trust in You always, and I know that my ways may not always be Your ways, and I know that Your way is better than my way. May I never put You to the test.

Genesis 28:10-22a

July 7, 2015

How hard is it for you to change who you are? Sometimes God changes us against our human will. Today's reading we see Jacob wrestling with an Angel. He is fighting the will of God. When they are done, God changes his name from Jacob to Israel. Israel is now a new person, someone God can work with. We see many times in the Bible when God wants to use someone He changes their name. Abraham was Abram, Israel was Jacob, Peter was Simon, and Paul was Saul, just to name a few. God changed them to be something better, and changed their names, usually after some sort of torment, or struggle with their former self. Are you still wrestling with God, because you don't want to change who you are? Is God making you into something great, and you are resisting it? Who wins this battle in the end? Do you let God change your life, and everything about who you were, or do you allow the things of this world to keep you who you are, and not strive to become more? Will God win, or will you allow Satan to hold on to your soul, in this world?

Lord, I give you everything of who I was, but sometimes I am weak, and do not let go of the past. Make me that new person, the one that knows only Your goodness, and Grace.

Genesis 32:23-33

July 8, 2015

Are you strong enough to go into the world, your workplace, your school, your home, and gather the lost souls for Jesus Christ? Do you know what you need to know to accomplish it? The 12 Apostles, that Jesus chose, were no different than you and I. They were not the rich, the highly educated, or even the most outgoing people of their time. They were ordinary people that Jesus showed how to accomplish what He was calling them to do. This was not the beginning of Jesus' ministry, so they had already witnessed some of the miracles He was performing. They knew He was driving out demons, with the authority of God. Were they capable? Did they think they could do it? Jesus gave them the authority, and they had to trust Him, after all they had seen, they knew He was the Son of God. Do you have what it takes to tell people the kingdom of God is at hand? We may say we do, but there is an internal fear that we have, that someone may say something that we won't know how to handle, or we may think this is not where I'm comfortable. How hard is it for us to call the Holy Spirit to guide our way? You can do it, He will help, and you just need to ask Him to guide you. Are your friends and family worth it?

Holy Spirit come and guide me through my day that I may show those that are lost the way to know our Father more fully, and know that He is all Love, and wants them to know Him.

Matt 10:1-7

July 9, 2015

How do you handle the situations that you can't control? Do you get mad, and blame others for the things that are happening to you? Do you look at the situation, and see that God may have put you there for a purpose? Joseph was the son of Israel (Jacob), and he had dreams that he shared with his brother's, that they didn't like. They didn't like them because his dreams showed him in a position of power, and his brothers were all older then him. The brothers sold him to the Egyptians, to be a slave. Joseph didn't hold a grudge against his brother's, he knew there was a reason he was where he was. He became slightly less in power, than the pharaohs. How do you handle the challenges thrown at you each day? Do you press on, and know that God is with you, or do you melt into your own world, and take people with you?

Lord, may I always know You are with me, and know that I am where I am, because there is a purpose. Help me to have the strength to get through those times.

Gen 44:18-21, 23b-29; 45:1-5

July 10, 2015

Have you ever been in sports, where you had a coach that was very motivating? How about going to see a motivational speaker? They do everything in their power to motivate you to do for the team, or do it for yourself. Life will be better for you, and for those around you if you go out there and "just do it". Jesus uses a different tactic. He tells them the way it will be. He wants people that will do what He is asking them to do, no matter what the consequences are. People will hate you. Parents will accuse their children. The children will accuse their parents. That doesn't sound like a motivational speaker to me. Why is he considered one of the greatest leaders of all time? Why do so many people follow Him? Because it's not about you, or the people. That's not who we are trying to impress. It is about letting people know about their own salvation, at any cost. He told them the truth, and wants us to do the same. We shouldn't fear persecution, it will happen. We shouldn't fear what to say in our defense. We should call on the Holy Spirit, and He will provide the words needed. Why do we have fear to speak of Jesus Christ? Isn't it all about our salvation, and everyone else's? What is your motivation?

Lord, You alone can give everlasting life, may I go into the world, and know that you are with me, and will provide me the words, through the Holy Spirit.

Matt 10:16-23

189

July 11, 2015

What do you fear? Who do you fear? We all have fears that make us suffer, if we are consumed by those fears. Do you dwell on them? Jesus is still in the process of sending out the disciples to show the world, through miracles and teaching, that God is a God of love, and He will be with you, as long as you trust in Him. He provides us with the strength and courage we need, if we only trust. Jesus is very adamant that we are far better off to lose our life, than we are to lose our soul. Why do so many people say there is a Heaven, but deny there is a Hell? Can there be one without the other? Why should there be a Heaven, if there is no alternative place to end up? Sometimes we think of this world as Hell, and think that there can't be something worse. Wouldn't Hell be a complete absence of God? If God is love, and there is no love, wouldn't that be the definition of Hell? This world has love in it, because there are people in it, to show love. Can you imagine a place that has zero love for you, or anyone else in it? Wouldn't that be Hell? Why would we not want to go out and show the love God has to offer, over the alternative? Do you fear losing your soul? How about the souls of those you are close to?

Lord, You do not encourage us by fear, you encourage us by love, may I be an example of that love you have shown to me. May people see You in me.

Matt 10:24-33

190

July12, 2015

When you try to talk about your faith to someone, do they always accept, or welcome it? What do you do if they don't? Do you stay there and argue with them? Jesus instructs the twelve Apostles to go out, two by two, and take nothing extra with them. He tells them if someone accepts you, to stay there, but more importantly he tells them, if someone does not accept what you are telling them, that you should leave, and shake the dust from your feet. If they don't like what you are saying, don't stay there, and don't let them hang onto you, and slow you down. Sales is like that. If you want to be successful, you can't think about the person that had every reason in the book to not buy what your selling, you just have to move on to the next place and not think about the reasons the last person didn't want it. If you dwell on the negative, it is very hard to stay positive. Not everyone is going to want what Jesus has done for us. Sometimes you have to move on, and just pray for that person. How do you handle adversity? Do you give up, or do you just keep pressing on, knowing what you're doing, is right?

Lord, may I never give up the journey that you have sent me on. May I always know when to move on?

Mark 6:7-13

July 13, 2015

Why would Jesus say He brings a sword instead of bringing peace? Is He encouraging violence? Every day we talk to friends, family, and relatives, even total strangers, yet we ignore the belief system they are talking about. Why don't we take the opportunity to talk to those that believe it's all about "mother earth", or how they were a certain thing, or person in a different life? Is that what you believe? Do you love that person, more than God? Maybe that is what Jesus is talking about when he says, "Do not think that I have come to bring peace upon the earth. I have come to bring not peace but the sword"(Matthew 10:34). It is about the spiritual battle that we face every day. We see it, and we are afraid of offending a family member, friend, or stranger, so we just ignore it. We take risks every day, but we are afraid to risk a relationship for what we believe, even if it offends God. I'm not encouraging you to go start a fight with everyone you know, I'm suggesting that we need to be more aware of what is happening around us, and try to question the belief system that goes against God, and the love that is Jesus Christ. Will you bring the sword to do battle with the evil that is trying to minimize God, and make everything OK, as long as it makes them feel good? Who do you love more?

Lord, You provide me with the weapons to fight the evil that is trying to minimize You, may I have the courage and strength to wield them.

Matthew 10:34—11:1

July 14, 2015

If God was to judge the people on the actions of a whole town, to determine whether or not it was saved, would your town make the cut? Have you ever really thought about that? I'm sure you can think of people that may not make the cut, but I'm also sure you can think of people that most definitely will make it. But, what if God based it on the majority of the people? Are you the type that thinks most, if not all, people are going to Heaven, or do you think most will not make it, because of what you believe, or they believe? If you can think of a few, or a lot of people that you don't think will be saved to Heaven, what are you doing to change that? Is it your responsibility to make a difference? Shouldn't you be doing everything in your power to bring them with you? Do you care for their souls? If you don't, are you sure you are going to make it to Heaven? Jesus was in Chorazin and Bethsaida, and performed miracles there, and yet they still did not repent. Some will see and still not believe, and you cannot change that, but is that for you to determine? Shouldn't you still try? What will you do to make a difference in your town? Will it be enough?

Lord, You know firsthand the souls that can be saved, and cannot, but it doesn't stop You from providing them the opportunity to change their ways. May I be Your hands and feet, to make a difference.

Matthew 11:20-24

July 15, 2015

Have you ever experienced God in your everyday routine, when you weren't expecting it? Think about the times you were driving, or walking, and saw a beautiful sunrise, or sunset. What about when you see a child in the loving arms of a parent? Moses was working, and doing nothing to look for God, yet God called him by name, and he saw God in a burning Bush. God called him to save his people from the grip of Egypt, who had made them into slaves, after Joseph had brought them there to provide them food during a great drought. Moses was no one special. He wasn't a great speaker, he had a stutter. He had even killed an Egyptian soldier for whipping a fellow Israelite, and buried him to cover up his crime. These were the children of Jacob, whose name was changed to Israel. When God comes to you, do you hear His voice, and do you recognize Him? When you recognize Him, do you do Him the honor of speaking to Him, and more importantly, listening to Him? What is God asking of you? Take some time today, and notice where God is present in your life, and how He speaks to you.

Lord may I recognize You in other people, and the world You show me. When I hear Your voice, may I stop and listen to what you have to say.

Exodus 3:1-6, 9-12

July 16, 2015

How often do you feel like you have to go it alone? Sometimes it seems like when we are going through the toughest part of our life, or our day, we are the loneliest. We stress because we think no one is there to help. In today's reading, Jesus talks about reducing that burden by allowing Him to be yoked with you. A yoke was used to join two oxen together, and they were built specifically for the two oxen that were being joined. When we are yoked with Jesus we allow Him to bare some of the burden. We aren't alone, and we don't have to go it alone. Sometimes, our pride doesn't like to share that burden, because we are "strong" and we don't need the help. We have to allow the yoke to be attached. It doesn't just happen, if we don't allow it. Are you willing to swallow your foolish pride, and come to Jesus, and allow Him to bare some of the weight of your burdens? There is a great poem, called Footprints, if you've read it you know what I mean, if you haven't, find it and read it. Will you pray today, to have Jesus help you carry the load of your day?

Lord, so many times I try to be strong, and try to go it alone, because of my pride. I need to have You yoked to me, and help me with the times when I struggle, so that You will give me rest.

Matt 11:28-30

July 17, 2015

What are your Sundays like? Is it just another day to get things done, or do you actually take the day to go to Church, and relax? Some people have jobs that require them to work on Sundays, and have no choice. Anybody fifty or older, can remember a time when you had a hard time even leaving your house, because nothing was open on Sunday, not even gas stations. All businesses closed down, so people could have family and rest time, and go to church. Everybody took that time to get together with family and friends. There were a lot more neighborhood get togethers, and people knew their neighbors, because Sunday was a day everybody had off. Jesus and His disciples were plucking grain to eat as they traveled through a field, and were condemned by the Pharisees because they were considered working on the Sabbath. Jesus tells the Pharisees that they are working out of necessity, in order to eat. Jesus doesn't say it is alright to work on the Sabbath, He says they are only working out of need. Do you still honor the Sabbath day, or do you treat it like any other day? God made it for us, yet we have made into just another day. Will you try to make time for your family, and rest on Sundays?

Lord, thank you for providing us a day to rest, may we honor You, and remember You, and take the time to relax on Your day.

Matt 12:1-8

July 18, 2015

Are you in need of healing? What are your ills? Are they physical, or are they spiritual? We all have a need for some sort of healing. Jesus withdrew, to escape the Pharisees that were pursuing Him to persecute Him, and many people followed, and "all" were healed. Did only the physically sick and lame follow Him? Probably not. But all were healed. So many times we think that Jesus only healed the physical ills of the people. More people are in need of healing for their spiritual illnesses than realize it. We see the things of this world, and we are a part of them, but we don't realize how it is destroying our spirit, it makes us weak. How hard is it for you to follow Jesus on His journey, and be healed, when you don't know that your soul is actually been destroyed, by this world? We become accustomed to seeing worse things on TV, in the news, and in our own towns, that our souls are being destroyed without most people recognizing it. Will you follow Jesus and be healed spiritually? Will you pray for your own soul, and those around you?

Lord, I pray you open my eyes to Your ways, and see the world, that I may know the healing I need. May I be an instrument of You healing hands.

Matthew 12:14-21

July 19, 2015

Have you ever felt so good about a task you were sent to do, you hurried back to tell your boss, teacher, parent, or leader about your success? The Apostles were tasked to go out and perform miracles, and spread the good news, and because they were successful, they came back to Jesus to share their stories. Jesus wanted to hear these stories, and tried to escape to a deserted place, but the people that were taught were so excited to hear more that they beat Jesus and the Apostles to their place. Jesus saw the excitement of the crowd, and was so moved with pity for their wanting more that He had to teach them. This is how a good shepherd, leader, reacts when needed, he does whatever it takes to satisfy his flock, for their own good. Do you know that kind of love? The kind of love that Jesus gives as the good shepherd? If you are in need, He will not abandon you, he will drop everything at hand, and come to your need. You need only to call Him, and let Him know your need. Wouldn't the shepherd of a flock leave his flock for the wellbeing of just one of his sheep? Will you recognize his voice when He calls, as a sheep recognizes its shepherd? Will you call on Him?

Lord, I call on You when I am in need, and You answer me, may I always remember that You will never abandon me.

Mark 6:30-34

July 20, 2015

Do you need to see a miracle, to have proof in your own mind that God exists? If you see a miracle, will you truly believe it is from God, or will you write it off as some magic trick? Even the people in Jesus' time on earth were asking for miracles. Jesus was right there in front of them, and they still didn't believe. If you don't believe in God, a miracle probably isn't going to do it for you. When I was younger, I remember saying I wasn't sure if there was a God, but had a sort of belief that there was a higher power. I wanted a sign. As I have aged, I remember some of the miracles that I was part of, and never really thought about them as miracles when they happened. I saw God save me from my own destructive ways. I saw God save my child from the grips of death, after her birth, and then again when she gave birth to her own child. I believe there were a lot of prayers said in those times that I was not aware of at the time, even my own in some distant cry for help. We want a sign to believe, but sometimes they are right in front of us, and we still don't understand, because we don't believe to begin with. Our belief/faith helps us to see what has been there all along. Faith helps us to see the miracles that happen in our lives, but not everyone has faith in God. The miracles don't give you faith, faith allows you to see them. Do you believe? Do you want to see miracles? If you see miracles, would it give you faith, or is it the other way around?

Lord I do believe, and I see because I believe. Thank you for the gift of vision, and allowing me to see.

Matthew 12:38-42

July 21, 2015

Have you been baptized? Are you aware of all the symbolism of the water in baptism? Every year at Easter vigil, the night before Easter, this reading from Exodus is read as one of, as many as seven readings, in the Catholic Church. It is read to remind of us God saving the Israelites from the Egyptians. God brought them through the water to save them from the burdens of the life they lived under Egyptian rule, and saved them to the dry land minus the burdens of their previous life. Baptism washes us clean of our previous life and gives us a new life, and a new beginning. Do you remember your baptism? If you're like me, I was baptized as an infant in the Lutheran church, and have no recollection of it. If you were baptized older you may recall your baptism.

   Lord, thank you for providing a way to cleanse us of our original sin, that we may be washed and be able to be close to You.

   Exodus 14:21—15:1

July 22, 2015

Do you recognize people after you have been away from them for a while? Sometimes we see someone we have known all of our lives, and haven't seen them for a while, and can't place them. Mary Magdalene had not seen Jesus for only three days, why didn't she recognize Him after He had risen from the dead? Did His appearance change that much? She didn't recognize Him until He called her name. Was it because she recognized His voice, the way a sheep knows the shepherd's voice? Do you know His voice when you hear it? Is it recognizable to you? Do you spend time with Him daily, as Mary did? She was with Jesus, even until His death on the cross. She saw His pain, she knew who He was, because she spent time with Him. Do you take time daily to spend it with Jesus in prayer? Do you read the Gospels daily, so you can recognize His voice when you hear Him calling you to bigger and better things? Do you fear what He may ask

Lord, I hear Your voice, and know You, but sometimes I question whether it is You calling me. May I be like Mary Magdalene, and know You by Your calling my name, and do as You ask of me.

John 20:1-2, 11-18

July 23, 2015

Have you ever been forced to attend a meeting, or function that you didn't want to attend? Did you sit there wondering why are these people so excited about this, and you don't get it? When Nita and I got married, I used to go to church with her, every once in a while, and I didn't get it. As the girls got older, I thought it would be good for them that I go more often. I couldn't help but wonder, "Why are all these people here?" Then I went with more of an open mind, and started paying attention, and some of the homilies started to touch my heart, and I decided to join, and become Catholic. I got it! I knew why I was there. I started wanting to know more about God, and who Jesus Christ is. It didn't happen overnight, it took time to soften my heart, to accept what I was hearing, and then reading. My pride didn't want to allow what I had conceived as weakness. Jesus tells the disciples that not everyone that looks will see, and not everyone that hears will understand. Our hearts must be softened. I could have stopped going with Nita and the girls, and been like some dads that I see seldom attending church with their families, but I let God massage my heart, and open my mind. I let Him have me. Do you truly see? Do you truly hear God speaking to you? Do you want to see and hear? Will you allow God to enter? Trust me, it doesn't hurt, unless your pride gives you pain.

Lord, You have opened my mind, my heart and my soul to know You more fully. May I see, and hear You when you speak to me, and show me the way.

Matthew 13:10-17

July 24, 2015

How long have you been reading these daily reflections? Are you spending more time in prayer, and trying to help other people understand who Christ is, and how knowing Him has changed your life? Are you producing more fruit? Evangelizing is not an easy thing for us to do, because of the unwritten rule that you can't have a conversation about religion. Is the conversation about religion, or is it about faith? When you share your faith, people will listen, and some will join in. When you talk about religion, everyone wants to say how much better theirs is compared to yours. I get that, because we become attached to that religion like family. Today's parable, Jesus talks about receiving the word of God, and what we do with it. Some will hear it, and not go with it, because they let it be stolen away from them. Some will hear it and be very excited about it, and it will grow in them, but when tested, they wither away. Some will let the riches of the world, and other worldly desires consume them, and leave what they know is true. But some, will be like the fertile ground, and it will grow in them, and they will share it with as many as they have the fruit to feed. How has God changed your life? Has He made a difference in the way you live? Can you share it with at least one person today?

Lord I read Your word and and I hear Your voice, may I be a witness to the love You have shared with me, and produce abundant fruit.

Matthew 13:18-23

July 25, 2015

How often do you wonder what your purpose is, or if there is a purpose? It is actually scary to think that way, and you shouldn't dwell on it. When I was younger, and didn't focus too much on God, I used to stare into space and try to figure it all out. How far does the universe go? If it stops, what's at the end? What am I supposed to be doing? Is there a purpose? Not until I allowed God into my life, and let Him take control, did I get past a lot of that. Yes, sometimes I still think that way, but God has shown me a purpose, and I have a desire to fulfill it. I always wanted to be someone of power, someone that people would look up to. I even thought I wanted to be a governor, or president. We don't desire to serve, we desire to lead, and have people follow us, and look up to us. Jesus teaches us that it's not about that, it is about serving others. Have you thought about how much satisfaction you get when you do something for someone else, and they are extremely grateful? It gives others pleasure and we receive the satisfaction of knowing someone is better because we served them. How can you serve others, and help them to want to also serve?

Lord, thank you for helping me to see that even though I have wants, I get more satisfaction out of helping others. Thank you for showing me how to serve.

Matthew 20:20-28

July 26, 2015

What do you have that seems so little, that God can use to do so much? As many times as I've read this passage, this is the first time it struck me that the boy brought forth the bread and the fish. He was a follower of Jesus, and when he saw a need, he brought forth all that he had, and Jesus used it to feed five thousand people. I'm sure the boy didn't think he could feed so many with so little, but he offered it up just the same. Did this kid have more faith than the Apostles? They said they didn't have enough money, and wanted to disperse the crowd, "how can we feed so many people?"(John 6:5) This is the only miracle that is repeated in all four Gospels. The message is that, Jesus is the bread of life, and he has the resources to feed many. The boy didn't have the resources to feed all these people, but he gave what he had, and Jesus used it to do more than anyone could imagine. Do you give no matter how small the amount, and let God do the rest? The boy gave all, and many were fed. What keeps you from giving your all?

Lord, so many times we think we need all that we have, and hold back, but when we do give, You use it to satisfy the hungry heart. May I give without regret?

John 6:1-15

July 27, 2015

Do you care more? Do you feel like your heart has grown, over time, so that you want to do more for people? There are some people that seem like they have always been caring and giving, but not all people are like that. Some people need to have their heart massaged to make them more caring. When we use yeast in homemade bread and dough, it needs to be warm, in order to be activated. It increases the flour, sometimes two to four times its normal size. If it sits in its package on the shelf, it stays in its normal state. It needs to be activated, and when it is, it reacts. Our hearts are like that, if we never stir the desire to know God more fully, or want to know what Heaven is, we don't activate it. What makes you desire to know God more fully? Is it the same thing that will make others desire to know more? Is there something you can do to change someone else's desire?

Lord, may You grow in me, that I may desire to share Your love with others, that they may desire to do the same.

Matthew 13:31-35

July 28, 2015

Do you have a choice as to the people that surround you? We can say that we can choose who are friends are, but can you really choose all the people around you? I think we all have a little bit of a dark side, and some people may be uncomfortable with the way, we act, when you come right down to it. There are people that are truly dark, in their thoughts and what they do. Do you still have an opportunity to help them become better? In Jesus' parable about the weeds being planted by the evil one, the weeds will be harvested and burned, but do we have a chance to change the human heart of someone that seems to be evil? Does Satan have the ability to create a human? Isn't God the one who creates us as humans? If that is so, then all have God in them, and all have the potential to be saved, and changed. Who do you know, that could use a little, or a lot, of light, to help them see God more clearly, and not be consumed by the fire, but carried by Angels to Heaven? Are your roots strong enough to pull a weed, and not be consumed by the fire? Do you have the will, and the courage to do it, and ask God to be with you to give you that strength needed?

Lord You know those in the most need of Your mercy, may You be with me, and guide me, that I may not be consumed by the eternal fire, when trying to save Your children. Lord grant me Your strength.

Matthew 13:36-43

July 29, 2015

Is it noticeable that God is present in your life? Do you radiate God's glory? In today's reading from Exodus Moses' face is radiant because he is conversing with God. The people saw it in his face. Are you someone that comes into a place and people know you are there, because you bring about joy or energy, or are you the person no one notices? Some people have the personality that brings energy wherever they go, and some do not have that personality, so it is not easy for them. Many times I have been asked, "Why are you always so happy and full of energy?" Part of it is my nature, but I want people to know God is with me, and sometimes I tell people that. I have always thought that I don't want to be that person that comes into a room and brings other people down, I want to be the person that makes people smile or laugh. My wife has even asked why I do some of the stupid things I do. I tell her that I want to make people laugh, even if it is at my own expense. Is there something wrong with that? Is it noticeable that God is in your life, or has knowing Him not made a difference in your life? Is it time for you to shine with the love that is God? Can you bring a smile to the person that needs a smile or laugh to help them through their day?

Lord so many times when I have a bad day, I don't think about the joy You have brought to my life, and everything I am grateful for, may I remember You, and share the joy You give, with those I meet. May I shine for You.

Exodus 34:29-35

July 30, 2015

Do you ever sit in church, and wonder about someone you see there? Do you ever wonder how many are thinking the same thing about you? We go to church to be close to God, and to be more enlightened by what we hear from our priest, or pastor. We hear people all the time say, "the church is full of hypocrites". That is most likely true, but isn't it also hypocritical to say that, and not go to church? Jesus' parable about casting the net and pulling all the different types of fish addresses this issue. We should try and bring in all, and help them to see with God's eyes, and know Jesus and what He has done for us, and if that doesn't happen, it is not up to us. God and His Angels will do the sorting, we don't have to worry about who is destined for God's Kingdom, and who is destined for the fiery furnace. Do you do whatever you can to bring in all people to know God more deeply, and fully, or do you feel that is not your job? Doesn't the Old Testament and the New Testament both encourage us to bring people closer to God, that we too may be changed? We learn from the Old, and we are changed by the New. How else can we find this, without some guidance? Will you invite someone to join you? If you don't go, will you go?

Lord, thank you for showing that we are all in this together, and we can only do what we have been shown, may I do Your will, that you may be Glorified. Today I pray that you consider all souls before they are cast away.

Matthew 13:47-53

July 31, 2015

What is your family history like? We all have family history, and sometimes it can be to your benefit, and sometimes it makes it hard to be who you are. We were not always the good kids on the block when we were growing up. We played in the street, we ran around town like we owned it, we fought, and even when we got older it was hard to shake that reputation. Sometimes people think, because that's the way they were, that they must still be like that. Jesus went back to where He grew up, and people wanted to see all the miracles they had heard about, but they were skeptical, because they knew His family history. Even Jesus was not getting the respect He should have from his hometown because of His childhood and family history. Did the people lack faith, or did they have memories that made it hard for them to believe He is God's Holy Son? We know very little about Jesus' childhood, but He was a child at one time, and sometimes kids, or other relatives do things that people have a hard time forgetting, and associate with the whole family. How hard is it for you to change who you were, to be the new creation that God is calling you to be? Will there always be skeptical people, no matter what you do? Yes, but is that any concern of yours?

Lord You know me, and You have probed my every being, may You continue the work in me, and may I go forth, and do as You have called me to.

Matthew 13:54-58

August 1, 2015

How hard is it for you to do what is right? This reading from the Gospel of Matthew gives a perfect contrast. First you have John the Baptist, who called out Herod and his, now wife, Herodias, for their illicit affair. Then you have Herod, who was so infatuated with Herodias' daughter, that he promised her, whatever she wanted, and wasn't strong enough to say, "that is not a valid, or moral request". John stood on what was right, and paid with his life, and Herod stood on his weakness, and paid with his soul. So many times we buckle under pressure. We are afraid of what other people may think of us, and make bad decisions, because we fear the people. Why do we not fear God more? Doesn't God have the ability to control the destiny of our soul, which lives for eternity? Is it because people discredited God, or is it because they feel that God is a forgiving God, and they can just ask forgiveness for what they have done? Have we gone so far, that we don't believe in God? You can see the direction that we are headed, and it seems out of control. It seems so many people base their ethics, on what is right with a political stance, more than what they know to be God's laws. Are we more concerned about people than God? What do you use to guide you, in right and wrong?

Glory be to the Father, the Son, and the Holy Spirit, as it was in the beginning, is now and ever shall be, world without end.

Matt 14:1-12

August 2, 2015

Are you searching for the food that gives you life and purpose? The crowd of people had just been fed by the miracle of the feeding of 5,000, yet they were still searching for that food. Do you ever finish eating, and even when you are full, you need that one thing to finish it off? For me it is that one piece of dark chocolate. It's like it completes the meal. Jesus is the completion that we search for. So many people search their whole life for that one thing that completes them. Jesus gave us himself, so that we would be satisfied. We now celebrate Jesus as the bread of life in the sacrament of the Eucharist. Jesus completed this feeding, when He proclaimed at the last supper for us to take and eat, this is my Body which will be given up for you, and likewise, take and drink, this is the blood of the new covenant which will be poured out for you. Jesus is the food that gives us everlasting life, and removes our hunger for more. Do you know the completeness of Jesus in the Eucharist?

Lord, may I never hunger, and always know that You complete me.

John 6:24-35

August 3, 2015

Have you ever thought about your faith compared to that of the Apostles? How about how much you know about Jesus now, compared to what they knew when they were walking with Him before He was crucified? Jesus challenges them to feed all the people with what little they have, and they pretty much said it wasn't possible. We know now that Jesus died on a cross, and rose from the dead, and sent the Holy Spirit to guide us. We also know now what He meant when He said He would provide His flesh for us to eat, because of the Last Supper. Do you have the faith to feed 5,000 people, even knowing what you do now? Why is it that we know all about Jesus, and we have seen miracles, and we still lack that kind of faith? Is it any wonder the Apostles didn't think they could feed that many people? Why do we lack in faith, and why did the Apostles lack the faith needed to feed the people? Do you still not trust that God will provide? I have seen people healed that I have prayed for, and I have seen people die that I have prayed for. Is that why we lack faith? Is it because we will never fully understand God's ways? What more do you need to do to strengthen your faith? Is prayer a good place to start? That's where Jesus started, before He fed the people. Is that a good enough place to start for you?

Lord, I know my faith is weak, but You make it stronger every day, may I always trust that You will do what is necessary.

Matt 14:13-21

August 4, 2015

What do you allow yourself to see, hear, or experience? More importantly, how does that effect what comes out of you? Do you use that to lead people in the wrong direction? So often we hear things and see things, and we believe them to be true, because of where we heard it, or saw it. If the right person says something to us we always believe it, but what if they are leading you in the wrong direction? Do you keep your focus on God? Do you ask for the Holy Spirit to guide your thoughts? We can see and hear things, but if they change what we do, and how we act, and we lead someone to the pit of destruction, are we not also headed into that same pit? Where are you leading people? Are people following you? If they are, are you making sure you are leading them where God wants them to go?

Lord, You have granted me the gift of being able to lead, may I always remember that I am leading them to You.

Matt 15:1-2, 10-14

August 5, 2015

Is your faith strong enough to go directly to God and confront Him for what you think is right? Have you ever asked God why something didn't turn out the way you wanted it to? Do you bring everything to Him, no matter if you think it is minor? The Canaanites were descendants of Cane, who killed his brother Able, and were cast way from God, and His people. The woman in this story was a Canaanite, and challenged Jesus to heal her daughter as He had been healing other people. She was not afraid to go directly to Jesus, and challenge Him as to why her child was not to be healed. Jesus challenged her back, by telling her she was not part of the reason He was sent. He was challenging her to see if she had the faith, or was just asking for a favor. So many times we ask God for something, like we asked our parents for something, just to see if they would give in. We didn't need it, and it wasn't necessarily for our good, we just wanted it. When you have something that you really need God's help with, do you go to Him with it, and explain your need? Do you show Him you have the faith needed to heal, or do you bring it to God, just in case it helps?

Lord, You are a merciful God, and want to hear our pleas, May I know that You are there, and will satisfy my needs.

Matt 15: 21-28

August 6, 2015

Have you seen miracles, or been part of them? How easy is it for you to proclaim Jesus Christ as Lord when you have been a part of a miracle? Peter was one of the three that was blessed enough to be with Jesus as He went up the mountain and Jesus was transfigured. John and James were also blessed with that honor. See the Gospel of Mark 9:2-10. If you have ever witnessed something, you remember it in detail, and you speak boldly of it, because you know it to be true. You don't have to think about what happened, it is engrained in your mind. How easy is it for you to remember the birth of a child, or another glorious moment? You have no problem telling people what happened. Peter was able to speak of what he witnessed, without hesitation. Are you waiting to see that kind of miracle to speak without hesitation of your relationship with Jesus Christ? Can you relate to the Apostles that were witness to Jesus' earthly ministry?

Lord thank You for giving me the opportunity to be part of miracles, and showing me what it means to truly live.

2 Peter 1:16-19

August 7, 2015

Do you suffer from an addiction? An addiction can be anything that could be potentially harmful for you, that you have a hard time controlling. It could be drugs, alcohol, sex, gambling, or even gossip. For those that have had to go through treatment to help you recover from an addiction, you know that you are never really cured. Every day you have to battle the demons associated with that old life. You had to die to that life, and you have to take up your cross every day, to get through the day. The addiction never leaves you, and it only takes one moment of weakness, to make you throw in the towel, and go back to your old ways. You must die to that old lifestyle. It's a style of life that wasn't good for you, but you knew what to expect, even if it wasn't good. Even if you have not had to go through treatment to beat your old life, you know there are little triggers that you have to avoid. Have you died to that old self? Are you able to go on, and not be enticed by the old lifestyle? If it still haunts you, there is a new life that can comfort, and not destroy. Give life, and not take life. Will you lose your life, for Christ's sake? Will you pick up your cross for a life with Christ?

Lord we all have the demons of weakness that we try so hard to beat on our own. Be with me as I go through each day, to carry me through the days that I am weak.

Matt 16:24-28

August 8, 2015

Do you love the Lord our God with all your heart, and with all your soul, and with all your strength? Do other people know it? Do you enjoin it into your children? Is it evident in your home? In this reading, Moses is instructing the Israelites to live that way in recognition of what God had done for them, by bringing them out of Egypt. When people walk into your home, is it evident that you love and serve the Lord? I remember when our girls were younger, one of their friends said that everywhere they look in our house, they see Jesus. I look around now, and it is not as evident as it used to be. Do your children have the same faith that you do? So many times, as parents, we want our children to also love and serve the Lord, but sometimes they walk away from that. Did we instill in them a deeper love for God, or did our children see things that made them think God is not truly in our lives? As parents we have that when our children do not seem as faithful as we want them to be. All we can do is pray and hope that God is with them at all times, and that they know He is there when they call on Him. They will eventually call on Him. We all have weaknesses. How do people know you love God, with everything you are?

Lord, I offer up my children, and all my family members, that You guide them, and let them know You are with them always.

Deuteronomy 6:4-13

August 9, 2015

Do you feel like you have done everything possible to make a difference? Does it sometimes feel so overwhelming that you just want to throw in the towel, and give up? In today's reading Elijah is feeling just like that. Elijah is considered one of the greatest of the prophets. Some people, even today, in the Jewish faith, still set a place for Elijah at their table. Some are still waiting for the coming of the Messiah. Even Elijah, the great prophet, was ready to give up. He felt like he was not making a difference, and he was no better than the ones that had gone before Him. He was giving up, but God was not giving up on him. We don't always know what we are capable of, but God does, and he provides the food needed to go on, in Jesus Christ, who is the bread of life. God provided Elijah bread and drink when he felt he had nothing left, the same as He gives us Jesus in the Eucharist that we receive. Do you receive Jesus in the bread and wine of Holy Communion? Is Jesus' sacrifice enough to make you carry on?

Lord Jesus Christ, thank You for giving me purpose, and providing the true bread from Heaven that gives everlasting life.

1 Kings 19:4-8

August 10, 2015

Have you ever really thought about how a seed works? It can lay around and never do a thing. If it laid on a table, away from moisture and sun, it would do nothing, and eventually rot. As soon as it is put into dirt, and given a little water, it dies. After it dies, it begins to return to life, and begins to grow. It then grows, and produces much fruit. We are like the seed, if we never die to our old self, we just sit there and rot, and never produce. If we die to our old self-righteous self, we begin to be nourished with the newness that is around us, and we start to bare fruit. We will be nourished by the new environment, and we will desire to be more than we ever were. Have you hung on to the old life, and resisted the giving up of what you were, and who you thought you were? Why do we resist letting go of our old self? Is it because we fear any type of death, even if it is just dying to our old self? Do we fear not being in a familiar place? How hard is it for you to die to your old self? Do you want to produce the fruit that gives everlasting life?

Lord God and Father, what I thought was my life, was really just me refusing to die, thank You for planting me, so that I might die, and produce fruit.

John 12:24-26

August 11, 2015

Do you seek out the lost and lonely? Jesus' teaching on the one lost sheep should give us pause. The shepherd should feel good that he still has ninety-nine of his sheep, and has only lost the one, but he goes out after the one lost sheep. He doesn't want to lose even one. We should be thinking the same way. Every time we see someone who is lost, we should seek them out, and try to bring them back to God. How hard is it for you to see a person that is lost, much less to seek them out? Are you the person that is lost? Do you need someone to show you the way back to God? We all are from God, it's just that sometimes we lose our way, and sometimes even deny it. God does not want to lose even one of His children. Will you do whatever it takes to bring back a lost child of God? Will you seek them out, and help them back to God's most precious arms?

Lord help me to see your lost sheep, and grant me the courage and strength to bring them back to You, so they will know the comfort that is You.

Matt 18:1-5, 10, 12-14

August 12, 2015

Why is it that we have such a hard time confronting someone who we have had a disagreement with? Why does it seem so easy to go to someone else and tell them about our grievance, but not go to the person who offended us? We have all had a disagreement with someone at one time or another, but did you try first to work out with them? In this reading from the Gospel of Matthew, we hear Jesus teach how to handle disputes. We have all had them, and most likely still have a grievance with someone right now. Do you go to them to work it out, and then if that doesn't work, get other people involved to go to them together? It's interesting that Jesus gives the blessing to walk away from them, if they do not see the wrong, and shun them from your life. He is saying that sometimes we need to leave things alone that we cannot change. There are some people, and situations that are out of our control, and we can't change. Jesus finishes this with a teaching with a command to pray together. If you resolve the issue, or it isn't meant to be, do you pray with someone for understanding, and thankfulness? Sometimes we think this is the hardest part, to pray with someone. Is there someone that you need to work out a dispute with? Will you go to them today?

Lord may You guide me, and grant me the strength and wisdom needed to go to my fellow brothers to resolve any differences we may have.

Matt 18:15-20

August 13, 2015

Have you ever felt the relief of forgiveness? You know you did something wrong to someone, and they forgave you of your sin. There is an unbelievable comfort in forgiveness. Have you been able to forgive someone who has wronged you in some way? When you forgive, you relieve the stress from the person forgiven, but you also ease your own mind. Today's parable teaches a very valuable lesson on how sometimes we are forgiven, but we cannot find it in our own hearts to forgive. Is it because we still feel the pain for the wrong that was done to us, that we can't grant forgiveness, or is it because we like that feeling of some sort of power over the person, by not forgiving them? Is there pleasure in not forgiving, because we can justify our anger? How has anger ever really made us a better person? Don't we all desire to be better, and please God? Who do you need to forgive? Do you have it in yourself to forgive?

Lord thank You for forgiving me of my sins, and sending Your Son, Jesus Christ to die for those sins. I am forever grateful. May I have the same compassion for those who have sinned against me?

Matt 18:21–19:1

August 14, 2015

How often have you been to a wedding? Do you usually think it will last, or is there something that makes you think it will not last the test of time? I know when you go to weddings you shouldn't think it won't last, but face it, sometimes we think that way. Prayerfully read this teaching from the Gospel of Matthew. Are you the type that was always meant to be together with someone, joined as one flesh, or are you someone who was never meant to be married? If we marry, we become one flesh, and there is no way to completely separate flesh from itself. How hard is it on each individual, and child involved?

Lord may You grant the understanding of Your teachings, that I may see Your love for each of us.

Matt 19:3-12

August 15, 2015

Do you believe in the virgin birth of Jesus Christ? Do you believe the Son of God was trusted to be carried in the womb of a young lady, who was chosen by God to be that Holy Vessel? How did God determine who would have that honor? Was it because of where she lived and who her family was? He could have chosen anyone to do this, right? No matter who He chose to carry His precious Son into the world, and protect Him during His vulnerable age, should have some honor, right? The Catholic Church does not worship Mary as God or Jesus Christ. She is honored because she was chosen by God to carry His precious Son into the world, and provide Him the love a parent has for a child. Have you truly prayed for understanding of the honoring of Mary, or do you take the word of so many people that believe that she is worshipped as God? I ask you to pray today for understanding.

Lord thank You for using Mary, as Your vessel to deliver Your precious Son, Jesus Christ into the world.

Luke 1: 39-56

August 16, 2015

When you meet someone new, or approach someone, what is on your mind? Are you trying to figure them out before even speaking to them? Do you approach them with a song in your heart? How different would that be? I happen to be someone who is always trying to read people. Sometimes I look at people and wonder where they came from, and how were they raised. What if you approach people with the intention of making them smile or laugh, even if you have never met them before? Do you think that would change the outcome of whatever you talk about? In sales, you approach with a plan, and how to get them to buy what you're selling. What if your selling happiness, and joy? Wouldn't most people buy that? Try to approach everybody you see this week with the intention of making them smile, and see how much it changes you in the process.

Lord may I always bring joy to those I see, that they may see Your love in me, and You may be glorified.

Ephesians 5:15-20

August 17, 2015

Have you ever wondered what it would take for you to be perfect in God's eyes? The young man who approached Jesus was asking what he has to do to get to Heaven. He had observed the commandments, but if he wanted to be perfect to get to Heaven, he was told to sell everything he had, and follow Jesus. I have had discussions with people that do not believe in God, or struggle with Jesus being their Lord and savior. They keep the commandments, but are unwilling to follow Jesus, and even more unwilling to get rid of their possessions. Like some Christians, they keep the commandments, but are unwilling to be fully committed. Most of us are not capable of being fully committed, but God knows that, and that is why He sent Jesus to die for our sins. Yes we still need to follow, and observe the commandments, and we need to follow Jesus, and we should sell all our possessions in order to be fully committed to God, but God will forgive us our sins now that His Son has died for us. Are you willing to follow Jesus, to gain entry to Heaven? What do you need to give up, in order to be fully committed?

Lord I am so easily fooled by what I see as riches in this world, that sometimes I think they are more important than my salvation. May I have the strength to remove from my life the things that keep me from being fully committed to You.

Matt 19:16-22

August 18, 2015

Why is it that Jesus seems to have it out for the rich? Does He not like the rich? Nowhere does He ever say the rich are not welcome into Heaven. He says it is hard for them to enter. But why? Is it because when people have a lot of money they forget about God, and the ones who do not have money? Do rich people still pray, and serve God? I'm pretty sure you can name a few, as can I. Jesus says this, because it is so easy to be consumed by money, and think that it is all about yourself, and what has God done for me that I haven't done myself. We make compromises. We fall into the world that thinks, "You don't need God to make it here". That may be true, but is it only about this life? Isn't it about eternity? The rich need to humble themselves, the same as the rest of us, and kneel before our God, to gain eternity. They are no different than us. Note that even the Apostles, who had given up everything, ask, "What's in it for us?" Our human nature, not our spiritual being, is concerned about status, and riches. It is easy for us to want to be seen as more in this world. Where are your riches? Are they in Heaven? Is your God money and status, or is He the God of our salvation?

Lord thank You for keeping me humble, and allowing me to see that money in this life buys me nothing in the life to come.

Matt 19:23-30

August 19, 2015

Have you ever found out someone else's wages at work, and wondered why they are getting what they are, and you are getting what you are? It's never fun when they are making the same, or more than you, when you have been there longer, and doing the same or similar work. When you started, did you agree to the wage? Did it seem fair to you then? Why do we obsess over things like that? Why do you suppose employers don't want you to talk about your income? It causes disruption. We even struggle with the thought of someone changing their life at the last minutes, and God forgiving them, just as He did for you, a long time ago. Why should we worry? Isn't Heaven, Heaven? Your life was enriched because you had the opportunity to serve others for a period of time, and they didn't have that same opportunity. Isn't there joy and satisfaction in serving others? Isn't that the part of this life that gives us peace, and purpose? What do you do to give your life purpose in this world that involves serving people? Do you still need to find that?

Lord Jesus, fill me with your Holy Spirit that I may serve you joyfully and serve my neighbor willingly with a generous heart, not looking for how much I can get, but rather looking for how much I can give. (From my reflection on my Laudate app)

Matt 20:1-16

August 20, 2015

Have you ever received an invitation to a wedding, and didn't go, even though you didn't really have something else planned? You just didn't feel like going, and getting dressed up. Didn't the couple have to go through all their friends and relatives to decide who they would invite, and who they wouldn't invite? Weren't you then, one of the chosen ones, and didn't do the honor of showing up? Would that upset the family? Jesus was addressing this parable to the Jewish people at the time, because they were God's chosen people yet they did not respect God. So God invites all people to celebrate in the kingdom of Heaven. We are all invited to share in the love God provides, and join God in Heaven, but it isn't a given. God wants us to prepare our hearts, and be ready for the coming banquet. Are you prepared to enter into the Kingdom of Heaven? Are you thinking because you are invited, you just get to enter? Do you truly know Jesus, and live as He has taught? Are you dressed for the entry into Heaven?

Father most Holy, may I prepare my soul to be close to You as an invited guest into Your kingdom.

Matt 22:1-14

August 21, 2015

Have you ever really thought about what it means to love God with all your heart, soul, and mind? Isn't that like always knowing He is present, and always wanting to do things for Him, and to please Him? Wouldn't it be like when you see something that you really want, and you can't stop obsessing over it, to the point that every thought, and every conversation, that one thing is on your mind? Is God in your every thought, and action? How much easier would it be to speak about God when He is always with you? What about loving your neighbor as yourself? What if you don't love yourself, can you truly love your neighbor? What if God is always on your mind, and in your heart and soul, could you love yourself and your neighbor then? Sometimes the simplest readings bring on the most questions. How hard is it for you to have God always with you, and in your heart?

Lord live in me, that I may be an example of Your love, and be ever mindful of Your presence.

Matt 22:34-40

August 22, 2015

How hard is it for you to be humble? Isn't it funny how some people lack in self-confidence, and some people think they can do no wrong? Most of that must come from their parents, or the people they admire the most. Sometimes being humble is very easy, but there are times when I can be extremely the opposite. I know communications equipment very well, and I can have a certain arrogance about how much I know, at times. I am also very competitive, and that comes out. Then when it comes to something I don't know, I am not afraid to admit I don't know it. In either case, I try not to lord it over people, that I am smarter than them. Everybody has something they are good at, but do you point it out to people? In this reading from Matthew, Jesus points out the arrogance of the Pharisees by showing people that they are in a power position. Do you lord over people your knowledge, or control? Do you use it for your benefit, or are you humble in your knowledge and power? This reminds me of an old song, "Oh Lord it's hard to be humble".

Lord I thank You for the gifts You have given me, may I never hold that knowledge over those You put me in contact with.

Matt 23:1-12

August 23, 2015

How strong is your faith? Have you ever been challenged by someone who does not believe in God, or in His Son Jesus Christ? There are more of them than you think. This reading from the Gospel of John can give some insight into a reason why some don't believe. Jesus just finished His long discourse on eating His flesh and drinking His blood, and the true meaning of the bread from Heaven, and some of the disciples and followers left because it was too hard to understand. Jesus didn't call them back, and say don't leave. He let them leave, and said, "For this reason I have told you that no one can come to me unless it is granted him by my Father."(John 6:65) Do you have faith granted by God? When asked, "Do you also want to leave?", Peter responded, "Master, to whom shall we go? You have the words of eternal life. We have come to believe and are convinced that you are the Holy One of God."(John 6:67-69) Do you believe, and have the faith to follow where Jesus leads you, or do you walk away when the teaching seems too difficult to understand? If you do not go to God, to whom shall you go?

Lord thank you for the gift of faith. May I be ever mindful of the faith You have freely given, and never leave You.

John 6:60-69

August 24, 2015

Can you remember when you first heard about Jesus, and how He also called you? I cannot tell you a specific time or date, but I can tell you when I remember knowing He was calling me. Some people can tell you when it happened for them, but mine was more subtle, and not specific to a day or time. I can tell you when God called me to join the family, and become Catholic with the rest of the family, and maybe that's when it happened. Nathanael, also known as Bartholomew, was quite skeptical of Jesus, because He came from an area that was not highly thought of in the Jewish community. Yet as soon as Jesus told him who he was, he knew he was near the Messiah. It was life changing. Do you know when your life changed for Christ? Was it life changing, or was it subtle?

Lord thank You for reaching me, and using me to do Your work, and helping me to see You. May I be ever mindful of Your grace.

John 1:45-51

August 25, 2015

Have you ever wondered why some people stop believing in God? All people have something inside them that pulls them to God, and understanding, but some people will pull completely away from that feeling. They try to justify everything through science. The way the Pharisees lived their lives, with forcing laws on people and saying you have to do this, or you must never do that, did not bring people closer to God. People need to know that God is a God of love, and forgiveness. How do you show that to people? Some people will even say that being good is part of the human make up, that by nature we want to be good to people. Wouldn't God create us to be good and loving, since He is love? Sometimes they will use animals as an example, and how they instinctively do not kill, except for food, but didn't God also create animals? Wouldn't He do the same for them? Why would the Pharisees force laws onto the people that were so hard to keep, and try to use that as proof of your love and commitment to God? Don't you bring more people with sugar, and kindness, than you do with fire and persecution? How do you share God's love for you and for others? Is it by loving, or is it by fear?

Lord You are the love that all people search for, may You make me an instrument of Your peace, so that people will know You by Your love.

Matt 23:23-26

August 26, 2015

What if everyone saw you from the inside, and not what they see from the outside? Are you a different person than what you show most people? Most of the time the people close to you know you from the inside, because we can't guard ourselves from everyone, all the time. We all try to show the best of ourselves when we meet someone, but is that the same person they know after time? It is very hard to hide what is inside of us, and where our weaknesses are, when we are tested by hardships, and things that we really don't like. Jesus continues to chastise the Pharisees and Scribes, in this reading for saying one thing but doing another. God always sees us from the inside. Does He see a person of integrity, and honesty, with no hate? Does He see a person that is very bitter with the people around them, and full of hate? If everyone saw you from the inside, would the people that are around you now, still want to be around you? Do you show people what you want God to see?

Lord may I be who You want me to be. May I see people with Your eyes, that I may treat them with the same love and compassion that You provide.

Matt 23:27-32

August 27, 2015

Are you prepared, or are you someone who just wings it? In life, I like to wing it. Nita absolutely hates when I say we are going somewhere, and I don't have a plan. Sometimes it turns out fine, but sometimes we wander around trying to find some place and we get there and find out you needed to have a reservation. Sometimes in life we can take those chances, but they help us realize that, sometimes we need more of a plan. What if Jesus was to return today? What would He do with your soul? Are you ready for His return, when He decides your destiny for eternity? What do you think it is? Have you gone to your neighbors and friends, and shared with them the love that is from God, and the salvation that is from Jesus Christ's resurrection? How about when you meet someone on the street, do you find out who they are, and share with them? How prepared are you, really? Are you waiting until you have had all your fun in this life, and hoping you have time to get right with God before you die? What if a tragedy happened today, would your soul be saved to Heaven, or to wailing and grinding of teeth? Is this where you just want to wing it? What can you do to prepare?

Lord God and Father, may Your Holy Spirit reside in me that I may share Your love with all those I meet, and prepare my soul for the coming that is You.

Matt 24:42-51

August 28, 2015

Are you prepared for the coming of our Lord? What do you do to prepare? This parable about the ten virgins is about being prepared. The first few times I read this, I thought, why didn't the prepared ones share? Don't we teach about that kind of kindness? In the times that Jesus preached on earth, the wedding feasts could last a week, and they processed through the streets all through the night with their lamps, if you didn't have a lamp and oil, you were not allowed to join in, and if you weren't part of the procession, you weren't allowed into the wedding. Jesus is telling us we need to be prepared, because other people can't share their preparedness with you. How do you prepare yourself to be ready for the final judgement? Do you spend time in prayer, and do you take advantage of the power of the Holy Spirit at all times? He is there to provide us the fuel we need to stay bright in our dark times, we just need to acknowledge He exists, and ask for Him to guide our words and our thoughts. How do you prepare? Will you spend more time in prayer?

Holy Spirit stay in me, and guide me when I lose my vision. Help me to be strong in my weakness.

Matt 25:1-13

August 29, 2015

What would it be like to be so hateful you would turn down everything you could possibly want, to have someone killed? More importantly, what would it be like to believe something to such depth, that you would be willing to die for that? Herodias had so much hate for John the Baptist because he pointed out where she was weak and lustful to leave her husband for another man. John had so much love for God, and who He knew Jesus to be, that he wasn't afraid to say what needed to be said, even if it meant his life. The two had different values, but John's cost him his life. Do you believe so deeply, and with enough passion that you would say what needed to be said, even if it could cost you your life? Would you really risk your life for what is right and just? How deeply do you believe and love God?

Lord may I have the strength to live as John did, even in the face of death.

Mark 6:17-29

August 30, 2015

What does it mean to be good, and where does it come from? Where does evil come from? This teaching from the Apostle James gives some insight to those questions. If all good comes from God, can evil reside there? Evil can only reside where God is not, or God has been pushed away from. We see so many violent acts in the world, and wonder, sometimes, how can they happen in a world with God who is all good. People have a desire built in, by God, to be good, but some people choose to cast Him out of their lives because they have seen evil, and give up on God. They allow the world to take over. Evil can only exist if God has been pushed out. Some people, that are good, can be affected by people that have pushed God from their lives. Can we make sure we don't allow God to be removed from our lives? Can we do good to keep God in our lives? What if we always have a desire to serve others? What if we pray for every situation, and be thankful for what we have? What if we acknowledge that Jesus came into this world to die for our sins and was risen from the dead, to show us God desires that we join Him in Heaven? Wouldn't we stop fearing death?

Lord may I see the good that You have brought into this world, and know that You are with me always, to bring light to someone who is seeing only darkness.

James 1:17-18, 21b-22, 27

August 31, 2015

How would you react if someone you knew, or someone from your town started preaching to the people? It seems strange that the people of Nazareth wanted to through Him from a cliff, but in their minds it was blasphemy. That wasn't tolerated, and it was usually a death sentence. Do you think that people can be that much different from who they were when you knew them when they were younger? It is harder to accept that, because you knew them, and may not have seen that in them back then. Have you changed since your younger years? Are you someone who people look at differently, now that God has changed you?

Lord may You continue to change my heart, that I may be closer to You, and trust in all You ask of me.

Luke 4:16-30

September 1, 2015

Are you someone who encourages other people to be better, and to not give up, or are you the type of person that thinks you can get better performance by fear? Some people do perform better when they are challenged and scared of a bad outcome, but most need encouragement to be better. I think most people cheer others on to get a better performance, but do you do that when you hear someone speaking of God, Jesus Christ, and Heaven? A lot of people are afraid to encourage because they seem unsure of what others may think of encouraging that behavior. In Paul's letter to the Thessalonians, he is telling them to not give up, and to not lose heart, but he is also telling them to encourage each other. Sometimes knowing the end is coming can be exhausting because we hear of it even in the biblical time, and it still has not happened. That doesn't mean it will not happen, it just means we need to be prepared for that time, and we need to encourage each other to continue on. Will you be a voice of encouragement, when you hear someone proclaiming God's word?

Lord, guide Your people to have the strength to speak of you, and not fear the people that do not believe. May Your Holy Spirit be our strength?

1 Thessalonians 5:1-6, 9-11

September 2, 2015

Do you seek out Jesus, and desire to be with Him always? Everybody that heard about Him, and what He did, searched Him out and wanted to be part of the miracles He was performing. After they found Him, they didn't want to leave Him. Do you do the same? Now that you have found Jesus, do you desire to be with Him always? Did the people that were healed by His miracles, continue to follow Him, when He was being brought in to be crucified? Where were they then? Sometimes we have miracles in our lives, and we want to do whatever we can to be near that experience, forever, then something happens that makes us think God gave up on us, and we forget about the miracle. We forget about what God has done in our lives to get us to where we are, and we stop following Him, and giving Him the praise He deserves, and thanking Him for what we do have. How easy is it for you to move past the miracle, and stop following Jesus? Have you had something in your life happen, that made you give up on God? Do you think He has given up on you? Do you still seek Him and ask Him to always be with you?

Lord be with me throughout my day, even when I feel I have it all under my control. That is when I need You the most to give me Your strength, and healing.

Luke 4:38-44

September 3, 20115

Are you a sinful person? Do you think God can't use you because of things you have done, or have not done? Peter has often times gotten a bad rap, because he denied Jesus, and He sometimes says things that probably make you have doubts about him. Didn't Jesus choose him to be a fisher of men? Didn't Jesus know he had faults? Do you have faults, and have you sinned? Do you think Jesus could still use you? I was never a real bad person, but I have sinned, and sometimes I still sin, yet God has called me to reach as many people as I can, for His glory. I am not perfect, and sometimes wonder if I will join God in Heaven, because of the way I act, or things I do. But I know God has called me, and He knows me, yet He still uses me to do what I do. God chooses even those who are not always the best examples of Jesus, but He uses those faults to reach people that may not have been reached otherwise. I no longer question God, or if He chose the right person to do His will, I just do as I feel God has called me to do, and trust that He will reach those He needs to reach. I no longer say as Peter said, "Depart from me, Lord, for I am a sinful man."(Luke 5:8) I welcome the challenges God puts before me, even if it means to go into the deep water, and fish where I don't think it will do any good. Will you follow Jesus, and do as He commands of you, or will you turn away?

Lord, I know You know me better than I know myself, may You send me to where You need me, and give me the strength and courage to do Your will.

Luke 5:1-11

September 4, 2015

Do you fast? Have you ever fasted? I'm sure there is a scientific explanation to why fasting causes you to focus better, and pray deeper. If you have never fasted, and spent time in prayer while fasting, I suggest you try it. You don't have to stop eating for many days, you can do it for a day. I would suggest a very small meal at some point during the day, if you have a hard time with it. When you fast, you starve your body for food, and for some reason your mind is more active, you are able to focus more clearly on those you are praying for, and go deeper than you think possible. The focus seems to be clearer. The Pharisees and Scribes questioned Jesus about fasting, because they had set days to fast and pray, and Jesus' disciples were not doing that. The disciples were very focused on God, because He was right beside them, in a way that the Pharisees and Scribes could not comprehend or even consider. Do you recognize God when He is with You, in the form of the Holy Spirit? Do you want to experience Him in a deeper way? Try fasting and praying, and focusing on those that need Your prayer.

Lord You have given me experiences that are hard to explain, but You still allow me to experience them. Thank You for the vision to know You more deeply.

Luke 5:33-39

September 5, 2015

For those of you who look for this in the morning, I'm sorry! It was a late night last night and a busy morning. It's hard when everyone gets up before me.

How many of you work on Sunday? It seems like there are more and more people that are required to work on Sundays, and you have a hard time making it a day for God. If you work on Sunday, do you take one of your other days that you have off, and relax and spend time with God and family? It is hard if everyone else has Sunday off, except you. Jesus and His disciples were being scolded for picking food to eat on the Sabbath, because in the Mosaic Law, it was a crime, and punishable by death. The law was put into place to make sure people took time out for God. Our world has changed drastically since then, but that doesn't mean God wants us to stop taking the day for Him, and for you. If Sunday is not an option for you because of work, can you take another day, and make it your Sabbath day? How do you spend your Sabbath day?

Lord, it seems harder every day to make the Sabbath Your day, and not try to get caught up with tasks I didn't have time to do during the week, may I be ever mindful of You on all days, and especially on the Sabbath.

Luke 6:1-5

September 6, 2015

Have you ever experienced a miracle? After you experienced it, did you tell anyone, or did you keep it to yourself? Most of us have experienced some sort of miracle at some point in our lives. By human nature, when we do experience them, we want everyone to know about it. We run out and tell everyone, because we want people to know that God has done something great for us. The man in today's Gospel reading was no different. Jesus told him to tell no one about his healing of his speech and hearing, and he told everyone. If Facebook and Twitter were available, he would have posted it. The people didn't share because they wanted to be defiant, they shared because they were happy and excited. How hard would it be for you to not share that kind of healing? What miracles have you witnessed? Have you shared them with others, to give them hope? Wouldn't that be the purpose of sharing a miracle? How do you provide hope to the lost?

Lord may I always share the love and miracles You have allowed me to witness, but not for my glory, but for Yours.

Mark 7:31-37

September 7, 2015

Have you ever wondered if Jesus provoked the Pharisees and Scribes into killing Him? I don't think that was His intention, but He did not fear them, and He did things that make you wonder. Could He have healed this man, out of their sight, or on a day other than the Sabbath? Yes. He did not fear them, He wanted them to know that the laws that they held on the people were over bearing, and it is good to do good, even on the Sabbath. When you have free time, do you go to the lost, and the forsaken, and give of your time to help them? Jesus never intended to break God's laws, but He wants to put some clarification to those laws. He wants us to know we can do good, and not fear God. Jesus didn't come to break laws, He came to give us clarification, and to give us hope. He wants us to stand up to the laws that go against life. Do you fear persecution? Do you have the strength needed to do what is right?

Lord, Your examples have made me strong, may I never fear those who try to persecute me for doing as You have shown me.

Luke 6:6-11

September 8, 2015

What is it like to be chosen by God to do something no one else will ever be asked to do? We have all been called by God to do something, and sometimes we struggle to figure out what it is. Mary was chosen to carry the Son of God into this world and, with Joseph, raise Him up to adulthood. In a way, it was an extreme request from God, but it also comes with the honor of being chosen for the task. There had to be both a comfort knowing that God was involved, and nothing would happen, but also a human fear of, "what if something happens?" Don't we all fear the unknown, and even if we feel God has called us to do something, we still lack the trust that He will be with us? Why do we lack that confidence, and faith, to do what God has called us to do? Thank you Mary, for your yes, when God came to you, for the honor of carrying His Son into this world.

Lord, may I have the faith to do what you have called me to do, and know that You are with me always.

Matt 1:18-23

September 9, 2015

Have you been able to completely remove the earthly part of your life, once you have put on Christ? Why does it seem so hard to let go of earthly desires? It seems we all have some vise that never lets go of us, and we cannot release. We can look at immorality, impurity, passion, evil desire, greed, anger, fury, malice, slander, and obscene language, and we can all probably identify one of those that seem to haunt us, and keep us from being in full communion with God. Is it because we can justify that we removed most of them from our lives, and we have a hold on the lesser one? Is it because so many of these are a part of so many people's lives that it is easier to justify? Which one is the hardest for you to remove from your life? If you have more than one, try to focus on removing them one at a time. There are times when it will resurface, but you will be aware of it, and will consciously be able to stop it before you hurt yourself, or someone else. We sometimes think that the only one that gets hurt from these is ourselves, but it can easily hurt those we love the most. Try today to focus on the one earthly desire that has been the hardest for you to remove. Pray for the Holy Spirit to give you the strength to release it, and make you aware of the times you fail.

Holy Spirit, guide me through this day, and be with me always to know where I am weak, and help me to be weak in my earthly desires, so You can be my strength.

Colossians 3:1-11

September 10, 2015

How hard is it for you to do good to everyone you meet? Have you ever really tried it? It is easy, even on a bad day, to be kind to the person that is always kind to you, but what about the person that never seems to have a good day, can you be kind to them? This reading from the Gospel of Luke comes right after the Beatitudes, Jesus' teaching on what to expect from God. God cannot hate, because He is all Love, and if you are all Love, hate cannot reside in your heart. Weren't we made in God's image? Why is it so hard for us to be kind to the person that is not kind? I have tried this, and it can make your day, when you see someone smile that, rarely, if ever smiles. Yes, there are some people that seem like the world has crashed down on them, and they require a little more persistence and kindness, but I challenge you to try to make everyone you see today, and every day, smile, or at least think about the kindness you did for them. It will change you, and the world that is around you. Are you the person that always seems to have a bad day? This will work for you as well. Try to bring happiness into your life, and those around you.

Lord, when I look to You, You never turn me away, You treat me with compassion. May I do the same for those I meet every day?

Luke 6:27-38

September 11, 2015

Are you perfect? How often have you been verbally critical of someone else for the way they handled a situation? Do you know why they did what they did, or said what they said? Sometimes we think the worst of a person, based on our experiences. We see things differently, when we are raised in different families, or different parts of the country, or in a city. We are exposed to different situations, and we are taught to handle the situation based on that exposure. The Disciples were being groomed by Jesus to teach the people about what God really wants us to do, and He wanted them to be able to lead without being critical. It is hard to do that, when you keep seeing the fault in others, but you don't recognize the fault that others see in you. Jesus also wanted them to learn, what He was teaching them, so they would not lead blindly. Would you want to be responsible for leading someone into the pit of destruction? That's why you should spend time in the Bible daily, and pray. Isn't that how we learn to be more like Jesus, and start to notice our own planks in our eye? How often do you read the Bible, and spend time in prayer afterword, to receive understanding of the scriptures?

Lord, lead me, so that I may not lead blindly.

Luke 6:39-42

September 12, 2015

What kind of foundation have you built to withstand the trials of this life? Have you taken the time to pray daily, read the scriptures, and live your life to be true to God? How hard is it for you to be always honest, in everything you do? Are you a competitive person? Is it easy for you to cheat, if it means you can win? Sometimes those are the most trying things. When you do your taxes, is it easy to fudge numbers, even just a little, so you don't have to pay as much, or get a little more back? Those are the foundations we build our life on. It's the little things that help us to withstand the storms that can give us the kind of hope needed to still be standing when the tough parts of life seem to be trying to take advantage of us. When we are faithful in the little things, no matter how hard it seems, the foundation of our faith becomes like granite, and does not wash our faith away. When we cheat on the little things, we make holes that seem to allow the bad to enter, and create the weaknesses that can collapse us when we are tested. How hard is it for you to be always honest? How hard is it for you to pray daily, to help you strengthen your foundation?

Lord, help me when I am weak, to come to You and trust in You for all things, not just when the storms are crashing upon me.

Luke 6:43-49

September 13, 2015

Who do you say that Jesus is? Jesus flat out asks for an answer from his chosen Apostles, who do people say that I am, and then He asks them, "But, who do you say I am?"(Mark 8:27) We all have ideas of who Jesus is, and some have different ways of expressing who Jesus is to them. Some people have said that Jesus is only a prophet. Some have said he was a great leader. Who do you say that he is? Is Jesus the Son of God, and the redeemer of our sins? If He was only a prophet, would He say He is the Son of God? Would a great leader lie, by saying he was the Son of God? How do we think of Jesus as anything but the Son of God, or a liar? Has God revealed His Son to you? Do you truly know His saving grace?

Lord Jesus Christ, You are my redeemer, and Lord, may I always be aware of who You are and what You have done for me.

Mark 8:27-35

September 14, 2015

Do you have a cross, or crucifix in your house? A lot of households have these, and it causes some to wonder why would you have that, to remind you of how Jesus died? Most Catholics, and orthodox Christians have crucifixes (the cross with Jesus still on it) in their houses to remind them of what Jesus did for each one of us. Some people think this is not the image that they want visible, because Jesus is better viewed as the risen Christ. I have attached the reading from the book of Numbers, when Moses was commanded to mount a snake on a pole for the people to be healed that were bitten by poisonous snakes. They were healed by looking at the snake mounted on the pole. Jesus references that same moment in this reading from the Gospel of John. If God would heal people by having them look up at a snake on a pole, wouldn't He do the same for people that looked to Jesus' sacrifice on the cross? What does the cross of Jesus' crucifixion mean to you? Do you see the sacrifice of life, for your soul, or only death?

Lord, thank You for the life You have given me, and the sacrifice for my life, and my soul.

John 3:13-17 (Number 21:4-9 NAB Revised Edition)

From Mount Hor they set out by way of the Red Sea, to bypass the land of Edom, but the people's patience was worn out by the journey; so the people complained against God and Moses, "Why have you brought us up from Egypt to die in the wilderness, where there is no food or water? We are disgusted with this wretched food!" So the LORD sent among the people seraph serpents, which bite the people so that many of the Israelites died. Then the people came to Moses and said, "We have sinned in complaining against the LORD and you. Pray to the LORD to take the serpents from us." So Moses prayed for the people, and the LORD said to Moses: Make a seraph and mount it on a pole, and everyone who has been bitten will look at it and recover. Accordingly Moses made a bronze serpent* and mounted it on a pole, and whenever the serpent bit someone, the person looked at the bronze serpent and recovered.

September 15, 2015

Have you ever wondered why Jesus gave his mother Mary to the Apostle John, and John to his mother? Apparently, Joseph was already dead, and you would have to assume that Mary had no other children. I know there are a couple references to Jesus' brothers and sisters in the Bible, but back in that time, anyone who was a close blood relative was considered a brother or sister. Could the brothers and sisters have been Joseph's children? It is held that He was older than Mary, by quite a bit. The Catholic Church proclaims that Mary was an ever virgin, and never had any other children, or sexual relations. This reading from the Gospel of John is the one used to make that argument for no other children. Why would Jesus give His mother to one of His disciples? Was it only because Jesus knew that John would take care of His mother, and be around to do it? Did you know that John was the only Apostle that did not die a martyr's death? John died on an island that He was imprisoned on. Was Jesus the only Son of Mary?

Lord, we can only trust that You reveal Your truth to us, and that we know you better, because of the words that Your disciples passed on to us. May You open my mind to understand.

John 19:25-27

September 16, 2015

Do you make things happen, or do watch to see what happens? If something happens, do you join in, or do you still just sit by and wait? In this reading from the Gospel of Luke, Jesus is stating His case against people that sit on the fence, because they are unsure. People that sit on the fence because they are afraid they may offend someone, if they take a side, are not who Jesus wants. He wants us to dance when we hear the music, and He wants us to feel sorrow when there is sadness. Sometimes I think some people are more open to showing their emotions. I for one am one of them. I can tear up at some of the simplest things of joy. Maybe that's why some people are called to go out to the people, they get a satisfaction by seeing the reactions of others. They tend to be able to reach into the emotions of others, maybe trying to initiate the same response they felt. Why do some people sit by and wait for things to happen? Do you go out to your friends and family, and share the love you feel from God, and the joy from knowing who Jesus is to you? Are you afraid of drawing attention to your flaws, or being questioned for what you say? Do you ask the Holy Spirit to go with you throughout the day?

Holy Spirit, May You guide me, and give me the courage to share the love I feel for You, so that others may join in that joy.

Luke 7:31-35

September 17, 2015

How would you feel if you were eating out, and when the waiter came to give you your bill, they said that your meal was paid for by some stranger? What if one day you went to make a payment on your house loan, and the bank said that someone has paid off your entire loan? Most likely, you would be elated by both. The free meal would give you reason to tell a few people, but you would probably change your life if you were able to live in your house with no more payments. Have you experienced forgiveness, in a way that is life changing? Someone paying for your meal would be day or week changing, but paying off a home loan could alter your life. Do you suppose that is why people that have sinned greatly, seem to be more appreciative of the forgiveness God gives us? How bad are your sins? How grateful are you for that forgiveness? Do you know the love that knows no bounds for forgiveness? Have you asked for forgiveness, no matter how severe, or how small your sins are?

Forgive me Lord for what I have done, and what I have failed to do. I am eternally grateful for the forgiveness You have given.

Luke 7:36-50

September 18, 2015

How many of us have been poor, or are still poor? What does it mean to be poor? Is wealth really what we all strive for? When Nita and I were first married, and started a family, at 19 years of age, we had nothing more than a $200 wonder car. We wondered why it even ran. But as time went on, we kept our jobs, and changed jobs to be better paid, and we purchased a house to raise our three girls in. We never really had a lot of money, but when the girls were all out of the house, it seemed like we had a lot of money, because we weren't paying for all the things you have to provide for your children, other than things for college. We learned how to save, and I learned I liked old cars. I think they're more expensive than kids. Where are our riches? They are in the times we struggled with being able to provide food for our family, and learning how to have fun without a lot of money. We didn't have much, but we had love, and a lot of time together. That is when we felt the richest. Does money buy happiness? No, but it can buy you a boat, or an old car. Those do not bring long term happiness. Remembering the times you struggled, and growing in love and closeness with your family, that is when we are happy, and feel the richest. Where do you find your riches?

Lord thank You for providing for our family as we struggled through the hard times, and the memories, and thank You for providing for us now and watching over us always.

Psalms 49:6-10, 17-20

September 19, 2015

How well do you receive the word of God, when it is presented to you? Have you ever really thought about it? We all hear it, or read it, whether it is daily or weekly, or rarely. Does it grow in you, and help to strengthen your life, and the decisions you make? When a farmer wants to plant a field, they have to prepare the ground, by clearing the rocks, and turning the soil, so they can produce a bountiful crop. Have you cleared the rocks out of your life? They are the things that get in the way, and only take up space. They do you no good. Have you had a shovel or disk turn your life upside down, to expose the roots of your weaknesses? When our weaknesses are exposed, we can deal with them. Have you worked out the clumps in your life to allow the word of God to take root, and grow? What do you do to feed your soul? Do you pray, and provide the water that nourishes you? Have you prepared yourself to receive the word of God? What can you do, to prepare yourself (your soil)?

Lord, open my heart to hear You, that I may provide You the soil needed, to produce a bountiful harvest.

Luke 8:4-15

September 20, 2015

Have you ever been so mean, that you wanted to see how far you could push someone before they broke? When I worked in a factory, we would get so bored with the day to day routine, that some of the people would try to see how far they could push a person to make them mad. You would hear them talking about what they were up to, and you would sit back and watch. This reading from the Book of Wisdom was hundreds of years before Jesus walked this earth. The writer is writing of how they did the same thing to see how gentle a person could be, and if God would keep him from persecution. What is it about our human nature that we will get pleasure of seeing torment in another human being? Would you want to be tested that way? How often is your will tested? How do you respond when you are tested? Do you call on God to give you the strength to withstand the persecution of this world?

Lord, nearly every day we are persecuted, as individuals and as Christians, may You provide the strength to do as You have called us to, even if that means to withstand the trials.

Wisdom 2:12,17-20.

September 21, 2015

Are you a righteous person, or a sinner? Who are the righteous people? It seems no matter how hard we try, we still sin, and righteousness is so far out of reach. We all have sin. Why would Jesus want us as sinners, to bring His word to the people, instead of the righteous? How often do you see the righteous person going to the sinner? Isn't it easier for the sinner to strike up a conversation with another sinner? Matthew was a tax collector, and considered to be one of the worst among people, because they collected the taxes, and lined their own pockets at the same time, yet Jesus said to him, "Follow Me!"(Matthew9:9) Has Jesus called you by name to follow Him, and to go out to the people you know, to help them understand what He has taught you? Why do we never feel we are worthy? Why do we always feel someone else more qualified should be going instead of us? Are you worse than a tax collector? How hard is it for you to share how God has taken hold of your life, and changed you?

Lord, use me, a sinner, to go to your people, and show them the love You have for me, that they may know that You have that same love for them.

Matthew 9:9-13

September 22, 2015

Are you a brother or sister of Jesus? What is a brother or sister? It is strange that, most times, there is nothing that can come between siblings, and parents. When the same blood runs through your veins you tend to be more forgiving, and tolerant of a sibling, than of someone not related. Jesus hits a point, in this teaching, by saying that His mother and brother are those who hear the word of God and act on it. He is not dissing His mother and family, He always respects them, but He uses the opportunity to make a point. Do you love your parents and brothers and sisters enough to know them, and to be forgiving of them, and more tolerant of them? As Christians, Jesus wants us to know God more deeply, and act on His word, not just know His word, and not act on it. He also wants us to love each other as brothers and sisters. Do you have a broken family relationship? What does it take to heal that relationship? When it breaks in the family, it tends to be more hurtful. Is whatever happened really so bad that you can't heal the pain that is caused by it, to you, and to the rest of the family? What is forgiveness, if you can't forgive a family member? Do you share the word of God with your family?

Lord, so many times we see family members that have made a choice not to speak to their own family because of something that seems so small. I pray today Lord that you open the hearts of those who have broken relationships, and help them to ask forgiveness, and heal their hearts, so they may know Your kind of Love.

Luke 8:19-21

September 23, 2015

Have you ever fell to your knees, to pray to God, in complete helplessness? What drives you to the point where you feel you cannot deal with it anymore, or it is out of control? In this reading from the book of Ezra, we find Ezra too ashamed to even look up to God, because the Jewish people were not marrying Jewish people. So many times we try to push through life, and feel like we have sinned so deeply that we are ashamed to look to God, like He will not forgive us. Sometimes God needs us to reach that point of complete helplessness in order for us to be healed. It is then that we are willing to listen because we realize it is way bigger than us. When we are defeated, we are willing to allow any kind of help. That is when God changes hearts. Have you reached the point of feeling this life has defeated you? Have you kneeled before God to have Him help you get back up? He will handle you with the love of a Father, and bring you to a point where you know you can always trust that He cares for you, and will always be there for you. How far will you let it go, before you ask God to help you get back up?

Lord, thank You for always being there for me, and bringing me back to my feet, when I thought I could no longer stand. Thank You for continuing to walk beside me always.

Ezra 9:5-9

September 24, 2015

Are you someone who is always looking for the next best thing? Does it seem like there is always something that you desire? Herod was the one who had John the Baptist beheaded, and now he was hearing about this new guy, and all the miracles He was performing. Herod actually liked listening to what John had to say, but his desire to please, forced him to have John beheaded. Do you look for Jesus, to find what is missing in your life? Do you see people who have made the decision to follow Jesus, and notice that they seem to have found the happiness you so desire? Jesus is present, and we do see Him in other people, but for some reason, certain people have made it seem like a weakness to follow Him. Jesus can help you to be stronger, in the face of trouble. Do you desire to have Him in your life, to give you the strength you need to get through those days when you feel weak? Do you desire to have the peace and happiness that can only come from knowing God, and the assurance of eternal life?

Lord may I desire only You, that You may provide me the happiness that gives me peace.

Luke 9:7-9

September 25, 2015

Why do we always want to know what other people think of us? Is it a bad thing to want to be the best at whatever you are, or do? I try to be the best husband, father, grandpa, sales person, technician, catechism teacher I can be, but is it wrong to try to be the best at whatever you do? When you try to be the best, you definitely do better. But we always want to hear from someone else, if they think we are good at what we do, or who we are. Have you ever wondered why Jesus would ask His disciples who the people say that He is? He is God, I'm sure He didn't need to massage His ego, as we sometimes do. Was He checking to see if any of them knew who He truly is? He immediately told them not to tell anyone, who He is, most likely so He could finish what He came to do. He still needed to be persecuted, and die on the cross, and raise from the dead, and ascend into Heaven to satisfy what the prophets had said about Him. He still needed to redeem us, and didn't want to alter what was to come. Why do you think Jesus asked "Who do the crowds say that I am?"(Luke 9:20) Who do you say that Jesus is?

Lord, You came to save us from our sins, and yet so many people do not know who You are or what You have done for them. May I strive to be the best at helping people know You more deeply, so they can say, as Peter said, "You are the Christ of God!".

Luke 9:18-22

September 26, 2015

Have you ever been in a class or seminar, and the person leading it was telling you something you really needed to know, and you just couldn't grasp the concept of it? When I was going through Deacon training, we had a Priest teaching one of the classes, and he was going very deep into understanding the concept of God not having to deal with time. This idea still makes my head hurt, because we are driven by time. When something is so much a part of your life, you have a hard time understanding it not being there. Jesus was telling the disciples He had to die, and be handed over to those that would persecute Him, but because they could not understand why, they could not accept it. Do you ever struggle with understanding why Jesus had to die on a cross? Have you prayed for understanding? So many times we try to figure things out by ourselves, and forget that we can ask God. Remember, there are some things we are not always ready for, and those will be revealed to us in God's time. That understanding of time, is pretty hard to grasp.

Lord, You know what is best for me, and You hold the key to understanding, May I be patient enough to know that I will understand on Your time.

Luke 9:43b-45

September 27, 2015

If you hear someone speak about God, and who Jesus Christ is to them, do you first consider who they are, or what faith they are, before determining if you really believe what they are saying? Why are we so obsessed with the group, or denomination someone is part of, or not part of, before we determine the value of what they have to say? In the Gospel of Mark, reading for today, Jesus allows someone to continue driving out demons in His name, even though they are not one of His close followers. He was not concerned that this person wasn't a close follower, He was only concerned that they were doing it in the name of God. We see all kinds of news about Pope Francis in the news because he is in the United States, and everyone has to weigh in on what he is saying, and what they think it means. Some because they like him, or they are Catholic, some because they do not like him, or because he is Catholic. Does it matter what faith a person is if they are bringing more people to Christ? Isn't that what it means to be Christian? Since this Pope became the Pope, there are more people in attendance at church, and more people volunteering to serve, is that a bad thing? Do you read these postings because I'm Catholic, or do you read them because I profess Jesus Christ? After all, who is it all about? Shouldn't all the Glory always go to God?

Lord, may You continue to bless all those who serve You, and may we learn to accept all who speak in Your Holy name.

Mark 9:38-43, 45, 47-48

September 28, 2015

Why is it that we desire to be the greatest in some situations, or to be the favorite one? Isn't that part of our competitiveness? Where does that come from? Is it from our parents and our environment, or is it something that was given us by God, during creation? Even kids that grow up in non-competitive households desire to be the favorite, or the best. This reading from the Gospel of Luke always makes me wonder why the disciples were arguing among themselves about who was the greatest. Were they trying to decide who Jesus loved the most? Isn't that like a parent loving a child more than another child? I'm sure it does happen, but isn't that more about the child that happens to pick up more of your characteristics? As a parent, we love all of our children the same, it's just different qualities that make them different. With children, they are ours, but Jesus chose His disciples, each for a different reason. Then Jesus picks up a child, the least of all the people at the time, and places the child in a place of honor. Children at the time, were only there to serve. Are we to desire to be the least among people? Aren't we to desire to serve, no matter the status of others? Isn't that one of the hardest things we can do, in our mind, but the easiest to do in our hearts? Do you desire to serve others?

Lord, when I try to elevate myself to higher status, help me to see why I need to serve, and if the higher status is to happen, help me to remember, I'm here to serve.

Luke 9:46-50

September 29, 2015

Do you believe in Angels? What do you think of when you think of Angels? Are they the little Cherubs you see with wings, or are they bigger than man, and look like warriors? We all have our own perception of what they look like. In this reading from the book of Revelation, we hear about the battle for Heaven, and the Archangel, Michael, and his angels defeat Satan and his angels. Here we see angels as warriors. Most times in the Bible, that is the way we hear of Angels. Do you think of them as warriors, and protectors? How often have you had to battle demons yourself and needed help? Do you call upon the Angels of God to help you in your battle? There is a spiritual battle being fought for your soul and mine. We don't like to admit it because people think you are losing your mind when you try to talk to them about it. Just because it's not talked about much, doesn't mean it isn't real. Do you pray for help in battling the demons that want your soul? Do you call for God to send Angels to help you?

Angel of God, my guardian dear, To whom his love commits me here; Ever this day be at my side, To light and guard, to rule and guide.

Revelation 12:7-12ab

September 30, 2015

How focused are you on God during the day? We all have our jobs and families to take care of, but does God take center stage in your life, or just in your prayer at certain times of the day. When you see a person in need of prayer, during your busy life, do you pause right then and there to offer a prayer to God for that person? Do you then remember that person in your nightly prayers? We can all say we have busy lives, and most probably do, but how important is what you do, compared to doing things for God? Yes, you have to pay the bills, but we all have those moments when we see someone in need, and feel like they need a hand, or a prayer. How hard is it to take a few seconds, or minutes out of your day to help someone, or pray for them? God asks us to give our all for Him, but some of us, find it hard to give the least we can give. Jesus died for us, He gave it all for us, yet we have a hard time breaking away from our daily regiments to give a little. What do you do to further the Kingdom of God? Do you give your all, or just enough?

Lord, may I always be aware of those in need, and offer to help, or pray for, those that I see throughout the day, that need my help, or Yours.

Luke 9:57-62

October 1, 2015

Are you someone who takes God's word to the people around you? Do you evangelize? In this reading from the Gospel of Luke, we see Jesus send out 72 of His disciples to go and preach the word, and heal people. What were they to tell the people? Jesus hadn't yet died on the cross, or risen from the dead, and redeemed the people of their sins. Have you tried to tell people about God, without the redemption of Jesus Christ? There is a God, and He did create the world and everything in it, and He can heal the sick, and He does love us as a Father loves His children. We shouldn't need Jesus to evangelize to the people, but what a bonus to add what He has done for each one of us. When Jesus was gaining disciples He didn't have His saving grace to tell people either, but yet, He is considered one of the greatest leaders of all time, even before His death and resurrection. Jesus told them to get rid of everything, and take nothing. Is that because we then realize what God provides for us, and we eliminate the distractions from our lives? If you are sharing God's word, do you worry about whether or not the people are receiving it? Jesus tells the disciples to walk away, and shake the dust from your feet, and not worry about them. Why do we worry so much about what people accept, and if they accept us? We should just go on our way, and carry on.

Lord, give me the strength to remove the things from my life that hold me back from focusing more deeply on You. May I never fear sharing Your Holy Word with the world.

Luke 10:1-12

October 2, 2015

Have you ever had a situation that seemed to have no way out, and yet you made it through anyway? How many times have you realized that you truly have a Guardian Angel? When I was young, and in my indestructible days, a good friend of mine, and I were driving home. I was driving, and as I got to within 30 miles of home, I must have dosed off. I woke up about 10 miles from home. I'm not sure how I got to that point, as I had to exit a highway, and turn towards Cumberland. For the longest time, I wondered about that part of the trip, and how I got there. Some will say, I was awake, but just don't remember it, but then why did it stay with me so deeply? As I grew deeper in my faith, and studies, I realized that it must have been my Guardian Angel that got me to that place. Why did I get saved from that potential tragedy? Why have some not been saved from the same tragedy? Does God determine who makes it through those situations, or do our Guardian Angels? I have learned to be more aware of my Guardian Angel, and to be more appreciative of it. Can you remember a time when your Guardian Angel helped you?

Lord, You have saved me to go to Your people, May I always know You have made me for a purpose. May my Guardian Angel continue to keep me safe when I am weak?

Matt 18:1-5, 10

October 3, 2015

Why was Jesus never really revealed to the Pharisees and Scribes, the way He was to the disciples? They were very deep in the scriptures, and sometimes added their own laws to God's word. But why didn't some of them also see the Messiah, in Jesus, as the disciples did? God revealed himself to the childlike, but not to the learned. Is it because the childlike are more open to learn a new way of thinking? Would the Pharisees and Scribes have done what Jesus commanded the seventy-two disciples to do? Would they have been as excited about what they were able to accomplish, or would they have thought it was all them, and a power that they could use against those that didn't trust in God? When our mind is formed to a way of thinking, it is hard to open it to a new way of thinking. Think about the people that are strong in their political stance, could someone in the extreme of one party change to be in the other party? It could probably happen, but it is highly unlikely. Jesus went to those that had not yet formed a view, and helped them to see Him for who He is, and not who the Pharisees and Scribes thought they were expecting. Do you have a formed opinion as to who Jesus is? Who is He to you?

Lord may I continue to learn and know You, as You want me to know You.

Luke 10:17-24

October 4, 2015

Are you married? Was God a part of your wedding? I have attended quite a few weddings in my life time, some in churches, some at a courthouse, and some outside. The ones I remember the most, there was a strong emphasis on God being present in the marriage. We were married at a young age, and in a Catholic Church, and I wasn't Catholic at the time, but Nita was raised Catholic. I remember the reading from Genesis 2:24, "That is why a man leaves his father and mother and clings to his wife, and the two of them become one flesh." No one ever said marriage was easy, but it seems like it doesn't take a lot to destroy a marriage anymore. Why are we so quick to move on and not remember that marriage is like our relationship with God? Don't we grow stronger together when we survive the rough parts of life? What if you threw God away, because He had you go through a struggle in your life? I know some people who have. Isn't our relationship with our family, a microcosm of our relationship with God? Nita and I, even have some of the same thoughts now. Friday night as I was driving home, I thought we should go to Bona Casa (a local restaurant) for supper, and when I got home, she asked me if I wanted to go to Bona Cass for supper. Is that what it means to become one flesh? Does your marriage reflect your relationship with God?

Lord, thank you for the blessings of marriage. May You continue to bless our time together.

Mark 10:2-12

October 5, 2015

How likely are you to stop and help someone out, when you see them in need? Do you set conditions on whether or not you would stop? I asked this same question in a post a while back and the answers were mostly what I expected, because mine were similar. "Everyone has a cell phone now", "it's dangerous", and "I would call for help, but not stop". These are all understandable answers, but in this reading from the Gospel of Luke, the area Jesus is talking about was a very dangerous area, because robbers would jump people on this road. Why do we concern ourselves with our own safety, but we are not concerned with the safety of others? What if the person stuck on the side of the road was a young girl, and her car was broke down, would you stop then? I know this cuts deep, because I'm not sure I would want my granddaughter stopping in that situation. But, what if she was the one broke down, and in need of help? Do you see how we set conditions? The priest and the Levite were also concerned for their lives, but the Samaritan stopped, knowing he also could be robbed or killed. He was willing to risk his life for a stranger. That is the message Jesus was trying express about being a neighbor. It's not who we decide to help, it is anyone who is in need. That is our neighbor, who we should love as ourselves. Will you help out anyone, no matter the situation?

Lord You know my heart better than anyone, may I have the strength and courage to help those in need, no matter the situation. May I be not so worried of my own safety, as that of the person in need?

Luke 10:25-37

276

October 6, 2015

Do you take joy in seeing someone, or a group of people that have repented of their sins, and have made God a part of their life? What if they were a horrible sinner? God forgives even the worst sinners, yet we are not always happy when we see some of them come to God for forgiveness. Why do you suppose that is? Do we think, because of their sins, they deserve to be punished? How great is their gratitude when they see God has forgiven even their sins. Jonah went to Nineveh reluctantly. He even tried to run from God, and ended up in a whale's belly for three days, because he did not want to go to Nineveh, where sin was everywhere. After proclaiming that God was going to destroy the city because of their great sins, the people repented, and God forgave the whole city. Jonah was not happy they repented. He wanted to see God destroy the city. Was it because he didn't want to look like a fool, or because he didn't think God should forgive them? Do you see the people that have repented of their sins, because of something you have shared with them about God's love and forgiveness? Does it make you happy? Why wouldn't we want God to forgive even the worst sinners?

Lord, may I see the joy in others that have repented of their sins, that they to may meet You in Heaven, for You created their soul, as well as mine.

Jonah 3:1-10

October 7, 2015

Have you ever been mad at God for the death of a family member or a good friend? Sometimes we see death that makes absolutely no sense, especially when it is a young person. We wonder why God had to take them, or why they were given such a short life to begin with. These are the things that will stop people from believing in God, or keep them from ever believing in God. Why do we obsess over what God does, or how He handles things? Doesn't He know what is best? Then why was the person here in the first place? Didn't God provide them the life in the first place? Jonah was very bitter with God for not destroying Nineveh, and then for providing him shade from a tree, then removing that same tree the next day. He was pleased with God for the tree, when it was there, then he was mad at God for removing it. We have the choice to remember what good God has done in our lives, or what has been bad in our lives. Do you tend to dwell on the bad, or do you look always to the good? There is good that happens every day, and there is bad, which do you spend the most time thinking about? Do you have good memories of the person you lost, shouldn't that be where we spend our thoughts?

Lord, so many times I don't understand Your ways, but I trust that all is for Your greater good. Help me to get through the times when I have doubts. May the memories be my joy.

Jonah 4:1-11

October 8, 2015

Have you asked the Holy Spirit to guide your life, and to show you what God wants you to see? Many have been confirmed in the Holy Spirit, but have you asked Him for His guidance? Some people have asked me how I am able to do these reflections every day, and how I come up with them. Obviously, I'm a little OCD, and that helps with trying to be daily, but I ask the Holy Spirit to guide my thoughts, and my words, and to help me know God more deeply, so that He may be glorified in what I do. Trust me, sometimes I am at a complete loss for what to say, and how to say it, so I have to ask for the words, and sometimes, I read them after, and wonder how I wrote them. I truly understand what it means to be inspired by the Holy Spirit. The Holy Spirit can guide us if we let Him, but we need to ask, and we need to be persistent. Do you have a gift to share, that will glorify God? Have you asked the Holy Spirit to help you use it for God's greater glory? Are you persistent?

Lord, thank you for the gifts You have given me, may I be ever mindful Your presence, and Your willingness to give when I ask.

Luke 11:5-13

October 9, 2015

If someone doesn't believe in God, they in turn do not believe in Satan, but if you don't believe in something, does that mean it isn't real? If you don't have God in your life, doesn't that mean you have allowed Satan to occupy that space? This lesson from Jesus, from the Gospel of Luke, gives a great example what becomes of us when we remove God from our lives. If you have cleansed, or repented of your sins, but you do not allow God to be part of your life, and the protector of your soul, aren't you leaving that space open for Satan to enter? If you say you don't believe in God, therefore you don't believe in Satan that does not stop Satan from entering your life. Isn't Satan's ultimate goal to stop people from trusting in God, and living for God, and making Satan your ruler? You can say that you can do good, and not believe in God, and that may be true, but isn't that what Satan wants you to believe? You are either with God or without Him. If you are without God, then who are you with? Who do you have protecting your soul? Do you fill your life with the good that is from God, or do you think that space just stays an empty space, and it will not be occupied by something that is not of God?

Lord, may I never fall under the belief that I can live my life without You. May You always be the protector of my soul.

Luke 11:15-26

October 10, 2015

When you see, or hear, the word of God, how does it make you feel? Do you feel blessed because it makes you want to live it, or do you feel overwhelmed because you don't understand? We used to have a big coffee table version of the King James Version of the Bible in our house, we probably still have it somewhere. Every time I picked it up and tried to read it I felt overwhelmed. I had a really hard time with the old English. I still like my New American version the best, because it is a good American English interpretation. It also has footnotes at the bottom for references in other parts of the Bible. Do you read the Bible daily? If you try to read it from cover to cover, you most likely will get bogged down, as there are some of the books of the Bible that are mostly laws. When you read it, ask the Holy Spirit to guide you, so you can make sense of parts that do not seem to make sense. There are stories that you will relate directly to, and there a stories you will have to read more than once to understand. The Old Testament is a lot of mistakes we made trying to understand God, and prophecies of Jesus. The New Testament is Jesus showing us how to live, and the building of His Church. Jesus fulfills the prophecies with His life, death, and resurrection. Will you take time to be blessed by God's Holy Word, and live and observe it?

Lord, thank you for providing Your word to us, to help us know You better, and to those who You have used to bring it to life for us.

Luke 11:27-28

October 11, 2015

What are you possessive of? We all have possessions, but what drives us to spend money, even when we don't feel like we have much? Do you spend a lot of money on your pet, your kids, your cars, your home, or even yourself? Do you have a favorite sports team? I happen to enjoy college football, and pro football, most of the other sports not so much. I have shirts for Ohio State, and for the Green Bay Packers, and when someone asks me for gift ideas, I will ask for those. I also have a lot of shirts that praise God, and request those also, and I wear them a lot. If I can praise a team, why should I be afraid of praising God? Why do we fear wearing something that praises God, but don't fear wearing something that may offend someone that doesn't like the team we like? Is it because we're comfortable talking about our team, and will stand up for it? Are we afraid we will offend someone when we wear a shirt praising God, but not when it praises a team? Where is your treasure? If you love something, you get to know more about it, so why not do that with God, and His word? Will you try to make God your most important possession? What can a team do for you that God cannot? Who or what do you love more?

Lord may I always be aware of who You are and love You more than the things of this world.

Mark 10:17-27

October 12, 2015

Do you need a sign from God, to know that He is real? Why do we always need proof of something, is it because so many people do not believe, and we need to convince them, as well as ourselves? In this reading from the Gospel of Luke, Jesus tells the people that He is the sign, but the people still don't believe. He was right in front of them providing signs and proof of who He is, and people still didn't believe Him. We wonder why it seems so hard for us to convince people of Jesus Christ and God, and Jesus had a hard time convincing people while He walked the earth. Doesn't God make His presence known every day, when we look into the face of a little child, or an old person that has the wisdom way beyond our understanding? Do we really believe we could come from some sort of accident of nature? How much harder is it to believe that, then it is to believe in God as creator? If there were some sort of "big bang" where did the particles come from that started it? Doesn't everything need to have something to start it? Wouldn't it be easier to believe in God than particles materialized from nothing? What has given you proof of God's existence? Do you truly believe, and can you share your story with someone else, about why you believe?

My God, and my Father, I truly believe You are the creator of Heaven and earth. And, I believe Your Son Jesus Christ was sent for my salvation, and forgiveness of my sins.

Luke 11:29-32

October 13, 2015

What do you do to clean yourself from the inside? We all have daily rituals that we perform to clean ourselves on the outside, but how do you cleanse yourself internally? The Pharisees were full of rituals, and did a lot of needless things, to show that they were a very clean person, in hopes that those who saw them would think they were clean throughout. Jesus points out that, is not what God wants, He wants us to be clean spiritually. If we give from the heart, when we see someone in need, and don't concern ourselves with whether we are paid back or not, we are giving from the heart. Isn't that how you clean yourself from the inside? When we help someone, and do not concern ourselves with, "how are they going to pay back their debt", we learn what it is like to give freely, as God gives freely. How many times have you thought, "I will do this, and God will give me great treasures in Heaven"? Is that why you do it? Do you think God will make your life better than anyone else that is in Heaven? Is that even possible? Isn't Heaven a place where there is all joy and no sadness? Why would one person be treated better than someone else, if you are in Heaven? Wouldn't that be closer to being on earth, where there is resentment for people that have more, and competition for being better? That sounds more like hell, then it does like Heaven. What do you do to cleanse your soul? Is it as noticeable as what you do to cleanse your outside?

Lord, You give freely to those who do Your will, May I not give to please myself, but to please You.

Luke 11:37-41

October 14, 2015

How much is your treasure on earth? Do we see our good deeds rewarded on earth, according to our works? We've established that no matter what we do here on earth that we will most likely not be in some better part of Heaven. Does that mean that our lives are better on earth if we do God's will? God does provide for those who do His will, and those who serve Him. Do you take time out of your day to acknowledge God, and to acknowledge that there are people here on earth that need your help? Do you help God, by helping those in need of that love that God provides, by serving them as well as God? God has never promised that we will never see tragedy, and suffering. He did create us to have hearts that see when someone is in need, and to know that we can always help in some way, but do we acknowledge that, and do whatever we can, when we see the suffering? You may not always think that what you are capable of, is enough, but when we ask God to be with us always, He will give us the means to help, whether it is by works, money, or simply praying for those that need help. Will you pray for God to help you see, and give you the strength needed to help your fellow brothers and sisters? Who are your brothers and sisters? They are all God's people, all that you see, are God's people.

Lord, may I see with Your eyes, and have the strength and courage to do what is needed of me, and not be afraid of what others may think of me. To You be the Glory!

Psalms 62:2-3, 6-7, 9

October 15, 2015

Have you changed the way you live? Some of you have been reading these posts since I started, and some have just recently started reading them. Has it helped you to see differently? Has it helped you to treat others differently? Has it helped you to think more about the things that God has been teaching us since the beginning? Do you pray more? Do you give more of yourself to God and to others? I know I have been blessed with a gift to be able to interpret God's word in a way that helps me to live my life more fully for God, and my hope is that God uses this gift to show you what He has shown me. My goal has been to always write what I feel God has blessed me with, and pray that God can use this gift to share with those that take the time to read them. I know I can sometimes get a little long, but it is sometimes difficult, to say so much in such a short space, and still have people want to read. I thank you all for the kind words and private messages, they inspire me to continue to share God's word with you. Remember, Jesus gives us the hope and the promise of everlasting life. He alone provides us the path to salvation.

Lord I pray that you bless those who are committed to You, and continue to try to make a difference in a world that was never meant to be our home.

John 14:6

October 16, 2015

Who do you fear? Do you fear your persecutors more than you fear what becomes of your soul? So many times we are put into situations that can make us look better for our bosses, family, neighbors, leaders, or friends, but we may not feel comfortable with what God might think of it. We sometimes do things that we know will not be okay with God, and we do them anyhow. God knows we will make mistakes, and He knows that we are not fully like Him, and sin free. He has given us the ability to learn from those mistakes, and ask forgiveness. He sent His Son for our redemption, we need only to seek forgiveness and repent of our sins. If you are too proud to take that step, then you face the one who has the power to send your soul to a fiery eternity. God loves us more than we can understand. Some have sins they don't think are forgivable, but God has the kind of mercy to forgive more than we can imagine. Why should we fear those that can take our lives, more than we fear our eternal destination? What does God know about you that you are afraid to ask forgiveness for? Do you think He doesn't know your sins?

Lord, thank You for the forgiveness of even my worst sins, may I never fear asking for Your forgiveness.

Luke 12:1-7

October 17, 2015

Have you ever wondered if your sins will be forgiven? Are you afraid to acknowledge Jesus Christ, when you are challenged? Do you blame the evil of the world on God, and not give Him credit for the good, and the beauty of the world, but give the credit to some other act of nature? These are the things that start playing with your ability to be forgiven. Isn't blasphemy giving credit for something God has done, to someone, or something else? Isn't it also blaming God for the evil that exists? We should never fear who God is and who Jesus Christ is. Who do we offend by telling people about God? The people that don't believe, in God. Who has the power to save you to eternal life in Heaven? Only God, not the person you are speaking with. Many times you are in a situation that will open you for attack, and you fear having to defend your faith. You never have to worry about your defense, the Holy Spirit will guide your words, you only need to trust in Him. Do you believe in God, and Jesus, and the Holy Spirit? Do you deny God? These are the questions you need to ask yourself. If you are praying to God, it is obvious you do not deny Him, but will you defend your faith, and trust in the Holy Spirit?

Lord, You alone can give everlasting life, may I always have the faith to trust You, and never fear those who do not control my final destination.

Luke 12:8-12

October 18, 2015

Do you sometimes doubt that God is there for you, because you see death and pain? Did Jesus see death and pain? Does He understand what we go through? He witnessed the death of a dear friend, Lazarus, and a relative, John the Baptist. Lazarus he raised from the dead, John the Baptist was beheaded because he did not back down from the truth, and held firm in his faith. Jesus saw the death of a young child, and He raised her from her death. Yes it's true that we cannot raise people from death, but God still does that. Jesus can relate to the pains and loss that we feel, and He knows our pain. He came down from Heaven to know us personally, and to give us the hope needed for our suffering. Didn't Jesus also suffer persecution, and death? Do you think He can relate to your own suffering? So many times we try to find counsel for our pains and suffering, and don't think to bring it to God. When you pray, don't talk the whole time. Share with God your pain and suffering, and then spend some time in silence, and listen. Try to remove the other distractions from your mind, and focus on what God has for you. Prayer is not always easy, because we are not always good listeners, but you can do it. Will you bring your troubles, your pains, and your loved ones to God in prayer? Will you accept His answer?

Lord God and Father, thank You for sending Your Son Jesus Christ to know our pains, and for showing us how to live.

Hebrews 4:14-16

289

October 19, 2015

What is rich? Isn't it different for everyone? I see people that are able to travel the world, and I think they're rich. I see people with nicer cars than me, and I think they're rich. Doesn't it depend on where you are? Some people may look at me and think I'm rich. Compared to where we were when we were younger, we are rich. I have friends that have been to, and lived in, third world countries and the people there have a whole different definition of rich. It seems no matter how much money we have, we never consider ourselves rich, because our definition changes. Sometimes it seems no matter what we have, we want more. Does that buy us eternal happiness? What if you died tomorrow, what would your possessions buy you? Maybe a nice funeral, but is that really your goal? What if a thousand people attended your funeral? Where does that get you, besides in the ground with all the other bodies? Where is your soul? Where is your spirit? Is monetary richness our goal, or is it spiritual richness?

Lord I am ever grateful for all you have provided me, and my hope is that I will always be grateful for whatever I have. May my spirit be ever in Your hands.

Luke 12:13-21

October 20, 2015

What do you do to prepare yourself for a trip, or for an event? Don't you spend some time planning the trip, making sure you have what you need, and making sure someone is taking care of your stuff? When I was in high school, playing football, I had a routine before every game. I would lay down and rest, and meditate on what I would do in each situation, and I would make sure I listened to certain music, and as it got closer to game time, I would try to get everybody else just as ready, or motivated. Isn't life a little like that, when we start thinking of our final time in earth? The problem is, unlike a game, there is not a set time that we are aware of. We have to prepare our souls. We pray, we focus on God, we listen to music that calms our soul, and we try to get all our friends and relatives ready, so they can join us when their time comes. What if when you got to Heaven, you didn't have to play the game that you were preparing for, you were sat down at a great banquet and were served whatever your heart desired, and you didn't even have to clear the table? What if, because you prepared yourself, and your friends and family, you were the ones being served? What is your thought of what Heaven is like? Are you preparing your soul, and those around you, for Heaven? What, if anything, should you be doing differently?

Lord, may I be prepared when my hour comes, to meet You and share in Your Heavenly banquet.

Luke 12:35-38

October 21, 2015

Are you addicted to anything? Do you feel like something has control of you? When we think of addiction, we think of drugs, alcohol, and tobacco. There are many more, for example, work, watching TV, sex, laziness, reading, eating, and games. Not all of these sound bad, but some people are obsessive, and they can let even the simplest things control their lives. Does that obsession lead you to sin, or is it leading you to righteousness? Obedience can also be an obsession, but it does not always lead you to sin, it can lead you to righteousness. Do you serve God, and God's people, and has it become your obsession? I have seen people go from having an obsession for alcohol, or drugs, and then turning their life around, and then being obsessed with serving God. They went from obeying desires of wickedness to being obedient slaves to righteousness. Do you have an obsession that controls your body, and can destroy your soul? You can take that obsessive personality and make it a good thing by serving God. Will you use it for God?

Lord You have the power to change what we perceive as bad, and make it be used for Your Great Glory. Use me to bring Your people home to You.

Romans 6:12-18

October 22, 2015

How hard is it to remove yourself from the addiction that has gripped your life? What is required to pull away from a life that you have known, and seems easy? There is nothing easy about it, because it requires us to give up what we think makes us comfortable and happy. Does it really provide happiness? Isn't there a freedom that comes from releasing ourselves from all that destroys us? There is a grip of death that is hard to break away from, but if we can release ourselves from that grip of death, we can experience everlasting life in the comfort of God. God's love is far stronger than our addiction but we have to be willing to let go of the addiction, and reach for God. God gave us the ability to choose, and He will not do it on His own, you have to be willing to come to Him. Sometimes that requires us to let go of even those that we think love us, but are under that same grip of death. What a wonderful thing when someone breaks that grip, and comes to God, they can then, with God's help, help to pull others from the wreck that they survived. Do you know someone that needs your help, and your prayers to let go of a life that is an addictive death? Will you reach out to them and show them the love that God has so graciously provided you? Wouldn't you want them to join you in the joy that God provides?

Lord I ask that you provide the strength needed to go to those that are under the grip of addiction, that they may know Your love.

Romans 6:19-23

October 23, 2015

Do you know right from wrong? Have you gone to those you have wronged, and confessed to them, and asked forgiveness? What do you use as your moral compass to help you know right from wrong? Doesn't a lot of it depend on what we see from other people, and how we see those things affect other people? If we see a friend distraught over something that someone has done to them, we tend to try not to do that same thing to someone else. That seems all too obvious. Don't we also have counsel from God on what is right and wrong? I'm sure we have all seen the cartoons where there is a little angel on one shoulder and a little devil on the other telling us what to do. Isn't that our conscience? Most times when we struggle to do what is right, we know what is right and what is wrong before we do it, but we still sometimes choose the wrong, because we want to see what happens. We tempt ourselves. We are still responsible for what we have done, and we need to pay that debt. We don't always want to pay our debts but if we don't, we have guilt that we have to carry. Have you asked forgiveness from those you have wronged? Is it because you are afraid of the debt you owe to the person you wronged, and you may be responsible for it?

Lord, thank You for dying for my sins, and paying my debt. May I have the strength to go to those I have wronged, and seek their forgiveness?

Luke 12:54-59

October 24, 2015

How hard is it for us to save our own soul? Is it even possible? What do you do to prepare yourself for your heavenly destination? Jesus tells the parable of the dead fig tree, but what is its purpose? When a fig tree is planted, it is usually given three years to produce, if it doesn't produce, it is cut down and a new one is planted. Are you producing the fruit that is for God's glory? Sometimes we see the person that we see has nothing good to offer, no fruit, and we sometimes feel pity for them. Do you try to help them become more, and produce fruit? The gardener in the parable asked for more time to see if he could change the outcome of the fig tree. Do you know someone that needs more time, and you can do whatever it takes to save their soul? Most likely the gardener had been trying to save the fig tree over the three years, but now, knowing it will be cut, wants to put all his effort into saving it. When you see someone that needs to be pruned, or fed, are you willing to go that extra distance? What will you do to try and save another soul?

Lord, only with Your strength, and saving grace can a soul be saved, but with Your loving mercy and Jesus Christ's sacrifice, all soul are worthy. May You be with me always and everywhere.

Luke13:1-9

October 25, 2015

How badly do you want to see? Do you want to see what God sees? Bartimaeus was physically blind and wanted to see, so he called out to Jesus but the people tried to quiet him. Jesus called him and he threw down His cloak, remember he was blind, and would have a hard time finding it again, but he wasn't worried because he knew he would see. How often do we try to get closer to God for healing, and people try to keep us away by throwing up obstacles. If we are persistent God will hear us no matter how many obstacles are put before us. Bartimeus didn't worry about finding his cloak after He threw it, he was going for vision, and trusted that Jesus would provide it. He already trusted Jesus, as soon as Jesus called him. Do you want to see as God sees? Do you have the faith to push past the distractions and obstacles that are placed in front of you? When you do get that vision, will you follow Jesus where He is leading you?

Lord, may my eyes be open to see as You want me to see, and may I push past the things and people that try to keep me from You, and follow You.

Mark 10:46-52

October 26, 2015

Do you ever wonder why God would allow us to suffer in this world? Why do we have to see suffering, is it some sort of punishment? The first thing you should ask yourself is, "Is this Heaven, or earth?" Even the best and most faithful Christians have to experience suffering. Why should we not have to suffer? Didn't Jesus suffer? Isn't He the Son of God? Isn't Heaven, where there is no suffering? Don't we come out of suffering a little stronger then when we went in? Sometimes we get through those difficult times and we realize we made it, and are able to deal with that situation better now. It's not that God wants us to suffer, it's more that we are in a place that suffering happens, and can look forward to a place without suffering and pain. We have a choice to make at some point in our lives to want to join God in Heaven, or continue into eternity with extreme suffering, and no way out of it. Is that why we see suffering here on earth, so we have the ability to experience the difference between what God has to offer, and what the alternative is? Will you decide who to follow, before it's too late? I choose Christ's light! I will follow Him!

Lord may I have the strength to get through the times when it all seems so overwhelming, that I may join You in Your Heavenly home.

Romans 8:12-17

October 27, 2015

Do you have a hope or thought of what Heaven is like? Don't we all have a little idea what it would be like, but we still have anticipation as to what we will experience? It is likened to Christmas or a birthday present. You may have an idea, based on what you may have asked for, or by the size or shape of the present, but you still aren't sure of what it is. Even if you have an idea, you still want to experience it, and enjoy it. Don't we get glimpses of Heaven when we experience the joy of someone we know, or see a baby laugh, or the beauty of the nature around us. Sometimes it's the little things in life that give us the hope of a heaven where there is no sadness or torment, and no hate. We won't notice, or remember the hard parts of this life, because we will be ever aware of the happiness and joy we feel in Heaven. For we have thoughts of a Heaven, without the bad of this world, we cannot imagine the joy to be experienced, or the beauty, or the spirits that we come in contact with. The people we know, the ones we didn't know, and the ones we thought we knew, but may have never known a part of them that was more spectacular than we could imagine. Oh the thoughts of what could be of Heaven. What is your hope of Heaven? Does it change your outlook on the days when you are feeling down? The next time life seems to be more than you can handle, take time to imagine a life without that hardship, imagine what Heaven is like.

My Lord, and my God, I am anxious for what You have in store for us when we join You in Your Heavenly kingdom, but I am also aware that You have things that You want me to experience here, before joining You, and Your angels. May I be grateful for where You lead me.

Romans 8:18-25

October 28, 2015

How do you choose who you spend most of your time with? Do you pray for them? Whenever I read about who Jesus chose for His apostles, it makes me wonder a couple things. Did they have something special to offer, that other people didn't? Did He know the outcome of their lives? All died a martyr's death except John, and then there's Judas Iscariot. Did Jesus know he would betray Him from the beginning? Most likely, since He knew He was going to be handed over and put to death, and someone had to hand Him over. Did Jesus treat Judas any differently than the rest, knowing that? Jesus didn't chose His disciples by just a random act. He went to the mountain and prayed, and spent the night in prayer, and then He chose the twelve. There was nothing special about them, when Jesus chose them, except maybe, that they would live and die for what Jesus was going to show them, and share with them. Do you have what it takes to be a disciple of Jesus Christ? What if you were chosen to be an Apostle, would you be able to live, and die, for what you believe? Would you be like Judas, and say, "this is more than I want to be", and try to stop it? Or would you be like the rest of the Apostles, and be unwavering, and firm in your faith, and willing to die for Jesus, if that's what it takes? Do you have friends that would do that for you? Are you worthy of that kind of loyalty? Pray, a lot, for who you are, and who God wants you to be, and who your close friends are.

Lord, may I have the faith to live a life that will honor You, and be willing to give my life, if that's what it takes. May those You have put in my life, have that same kind of faith.

Luke 6:12-16

October 29, 2015

What will it take to separate you from God, or from your faith in God? How strong is that faith? I have friends that had been church goers, and then something happened in their life to make them pull away from God. They watched a loved one die an agonizing death, they saw people die, that they felt did not deserve to die. Some went to college, and a professor, or another student convinced them that God can't be real, or that if you believe in God you believe in a myth. Did they truly believe in God, if they left? How strong is your faith? Do you believe in God the Father as creator of Heaven and earth? Do you believe in Jesus Christ, the Son of God, who was born of the virgin Mary and was crucified under Pontius Pilot, died and was resurrected from the dead after three days, and is now seated at the right hand of the Father? Do you believe in the Holy Spirit, the Lord the giver of life who proceeds from the Father and Son? Sometimes we have to ask ourselves if we truly believe, and if we do, could anything ever really separate us from a loving God? Do you have the strength to hang on in adversity, and know that God will never leave you? We can choose to leave God, but He will never leave us.

Lord God, thank you for always being there, even at those times when I thought I was abandoned, You gave me the strength to overcome, and become stronger.

Romans 8:31b-39

October 30, 2015

How likely are you to do what is right? When people are watching you, and you are told, or asked to do something, that goes against what you believe is right, do you compromise your morals and principles? I have done sales for about 25 years now, and if there were ever opportunities to go against what is right, that is a job that will test you. I remember a call from a man who had just had a fire at his business. His telephone system was destroyed, and he asked if I could inflate the price on the telephone system I was quoting, so it would cover the deductible. I told him I do not operate that way, and he pressed me even more, and tried to make it so I would make extra money off of it. After I refused to buckle, he told me he wanted to do business with me, because I was honest, and he could trust me. He said he was testing me. I'm not sure I like that he tested me that way, but I'm glad I did what was right. Do you know right from wrong, and will you do what is right, no matter the circumstance?

Lord, may You always be with me, and give me the strength to do what is right, and know the difference between right and wrong.

Luke 14:1-6

October 31, 2015

Do you ever feel like you're being left out, or forsaken? Did you do something so wrong that you feel that you can't be forgiven? In Paul's letter to the Romans, he can sympathize with that. Being a Jew, they saw that the Gentiles were being given a grace that they thought was meant for only the Jewish people. Sometimes we grow into that position of feeling like we're entitled to whatever we have, and that our friends are always "our" friends, as if we have been given the right to control them. The Jewish people felt that God was only for them. Sometimes we have a certain amount of jealousy that makes us think we have the soul right to something, or someone. We get comfortable with what we have, and we feel it is our entitlement, and we don't do anything to keep it, or don't want to share it. Sometimes we isolate ourselves despite ourselves. Have you grown so comfortable with who you are that you take for granted whatever you feel is yours, will always be yours. Do we really ever possess anything, or anyone? God will always love you, you just need to show Him you love Him as well. Isn't that what it takes in any relationship?

Lord may I never take you for granted. I know that You will always be there for me, no matter who I am, or become. May my love for You, be ever growing.

Romans 11:1-2a, 11-12, 25-29

November 1, 2015

Do you know the joy of our loving Father? Can a person truly live without God in their lives? I know there are people that do not believe in God, and seem to live a happy life on earth, but do they know true happiness? Thomas Aquinas said: "No one can live without joy. That is why a person deprived of spiritual joy goes after carnal pleasures." Does a person without God find joy in carnal pleasures? Is that where their joy comes from? What is the purpose of a life, if not lived for God, and the eternal Heaven that is to come? I understand that people that don't believe in Heaven, do not believe in Hell either, but then what is the purpose of this life? If it is to be good to your fellow man, then what is to be gained, except maybe a better fellow man? Isn't it easier to also be evil to your fellow man, since there are no real consequences except maybe death, and a final farewell? Wouldn't the world be a better place, if all knew a loving God and eternal peace to be gained in Heaven? If all knew God as Father, and creator of all mankind, wouldn't we all be better off, or is that Heaven?

Lord, I am sometimes anxious for the Heaven that is to come, but I know it will all be in Your time. May I continue to grow in love for You, and show others that same Love.

1 John 3:1-3

November 2, 2015

What and who do you fear? Why do we fear anything, or anyone, when God is with us? Psalm 23 is probably one of the most recognizable psalms, even by people that don't spend a lot of time with God, because we see it in a lot of places. When we walk with God, and we keep Him the focus of our lives, we should fear nothing. How reassuring is it to know that if God is with you, you should fear nothing, or no one. Doesn't God show us the peace that can be, and give us the strength to get through the tough times that can seem impossible at times? Don't our wants and desire diminish when we have God with us? Do you carry the courage and strength of God with you throughout your day, and know that even your bad days can be your good days, if you are with God? The Lord is my Sheppard, there is nothing I shall want.

Lord, even though I walk through the dark valley, I walk with You, so I fear no evil.

Psalms 23:1-6

November 3, 2015

Do you ever have those days when you feel overwhelmed by everything around you? Do you go home at the end of the day, and still don't find the peace to calm your soul? Do you take time out during the day, and just spend it in prayer? Try giving yourself 15 minutes a day to just spend in prayer, add more when time permits. Prayer isn't just about talking to God, and always asking for something. Rather it's about taking time, and reflecting on your day, and being thankful for whatever you have. It's about getting your mind to a place where you can relax, and listen to what God has to say to you. When you reflect on the day, the good, as well as the bad, your bringing it to God, and He will help you know Him more completely. Sometimes the crap that happens in our day, makes absolutely no sense, but when we bring it to God in prayer He can give us understanding, and help us to have peace with it. Do you find your peace in God's presence?

Lord, may I quiet my soul long enough for you to speak to me? May I always find the comfort of your peace when I stop to be in Your presence.

Psalm 131:1 - 3

November 4, 2015

What is the cost to be a disciple of Jesus Christ? Do you have the desire to do as God commands you, or is it all for what you can get out of it? How often do we find happiness in just receiving? Don't we find true happiness in giving of what we have, and seeing the joy that comes from that? This reading from the Gospel of Luke seems a little harsh, but it is more about planning. Jesus tells those who wish to follow Him that they must be able to give up everything and everyone, for His sake. Then he goes right into planning to build a tower and preparing for war. He is letting us know that being His disciple, could cost us everything, including our families, and life as we know it. A lot of people want to be a disciple of Christ, because it may get them a special place in Heaven, and they forget that Jesus tells us what it could cost. Jesus doesn't want us to hate our families, the way we think of hate, He wants us to, not have a stronger attachment to them, then we have to God. He wants us to put God first in our lives, and be willing to leave our attachment to our families, if that's what it takes. We need to be prepared for that. What sacrifice are you willing to make, if it comes to that, when you decide to follow Christ? Have you thought about the cost of discipleship? Jesus wasn't trying to scare you away, He is making sure you are prepared for the cost of giving.

Lord, may I be prepared for whatever the cost is to be Your disciple.

Luke 14:25-33

November 5, 2015

Have you ever actively pursued sinners, to bring them to God? We're all sinners, and most likely, someone brought you back, didn't they? Are we afraid of what might happen to us, or what people might think of us, if we are associating with a sinner, that is known to be a sinner? What is this life about, if it isn't about trying to bring people back to God? Every day we go off to our jobs, or to school, or off to some activity, and every day we have the opportunity to share our love of God with someone, but do we do it? Yes, we have to give of ourselves when we seek the lost, but the joy and excitement that comes from finding the lost souls is worthy of celebration. Do you go off to your job, school, or activity every day, just planning to do whatever the task is that is before you? What if you gave yourself the challenge of speaking to somebody about who Jesus is to you in your life, and they start asking questions, and started showing an interest in getting to know what you know, and all of the sudden started showing new life? Isn't that what gives us purpose? When it comes down to it, is there anything more important than saving people's souls? Will you give it a try, and ask the Holy Spirit to give you the words to say?

Lord, may Your Holy Spirit be with me as I go through this day and every day, to speak the words that give everlasting life, that I may see the joy in their eyes, when they find You.

Luke 15:1-10

November 6, 2015

Have you ever wondered why I take this time out of the day, every day to write these reflections? I, like some of you, had a hard time trying to figure out what the Bible was trying to say, and why it was such a large book to say what it did say. I searched for someone to speak to me so that I could understand what God was trying to tell me. Sometimes I wonder if that was God's way of getting me to do this. We are all given gifts, and sometimes God has to smack us, for us to see what they are. God helped me to understand, and wanted me to bring His message to people that wouldn't necessarily be looking for His message, where they found it. My goal has been to make the words of the Bible have meaning, and life to those who don't always understand it. Like Paul, in his writing to the Romans, the goal is to speak so others may understand. "Those who have never been told of him shall see, and those who have never heard of him shall understand" (Rom 15:21). May God's blessings be with you, that you may know Him more completely, and love Him more deeply?

Lord, I pray for all those who happen to come across Your message, that they may find answers, and understanding, and be blessed by Your compassion.

Romans 15:14-21

November 7, 2015

Can you be trusted with small things? If you were at a checkout, and your total is six dollars, and you give them a ten, but they give you back change for a twenty, what do you do? Does your answer change, if the person behind you, or a child sees you? What if you thought the cashier could be fired for the mistake they made? Does that change your answer, or was it their fault, so let them pay the price? If you have to think about who might see, or the consequences of the cashier, is that a sign that you cannot always be trusted in small things, therefore you cannot be trusted in big things? These are the little things in life, but they affect the big things. How do you react when money is involved versus when it is something monetary? If God guides your heart in the little things, won't He also do the same in life changing matters? How much faith do you have in God, and does He change the way you do things in your everyday life?

Lord, may I be an example of You, even in my times of weakness, and no matter who may see, love You more than money.

Luke 16:9-15

November 8, 2015

What does it mean to have nothing, and still give? To be so desperate, to be planning your last meal, for you and your child, and someone comes along and says, they want you to get them water and feed them? Most people would argue, and tell them to go find their own food. The widow in the story did neither. She went to get what Elijah asked for, and trusted that He was right, and she would have plenty of food, until the rains came again. So many times we are afraid to give, because we don't think we have anything to give, but I can tell you, when we give out of nothing, that is when we receive the most. If the widow would have argued with Elijah about how little she had, and not had done what was asked of her, she probably would have fixed her last meal for her, and her child. Our God is a gracious loving God, and He is always giving, but He wants us to also give, even when we think we can't afford it. No matter how bad we think we have it, someone always has it worse. Do people in third world countries, with nothing to give, find it easier to have faith, because they have nothing else to hope for? We have plenty, yet our faith is falling away. Do we have faith, only when we are desperate?

Lord, may I always have faith in Your saving grace, even when times are good. May I never feel that what I have is only mine?

1 Kings 17:10-16

November 9, 2015

Have you ever wondered why we go so far in trying to please our physical body, and mind, no matter the cost? Sometimes we do things that are only for physical pleasure. So many times we see people destroy their body by drugs, alcohol, and food. My biggest weakness is food. My dad used to tell me, "you don't eat to live, you live to eat". Food has been a weakness because I do like to cook, and I like to season. We don't often think about food as destroying the body, but when we over indulge in anything, we are abusing. Do you think if we realized that our bodies are a temple of God, we would change the way we treat it? Why is it that addictions and obsessions, consume our mind to the point that we can completely forget that our body is a temple of God? Sometimes it seems like we have no control. How often have you been pushed to that point when something that could destroy your mind and body, seems to overwhelm you? Do you think about your body being a temple of God?

Lord may You grant me the strength to overcome the thoughts that make me want more, and remember that my body is a temple for You.

1 Corinthians 3:9c-11, 16-17

November 10, 2015

Have you ever felt you were worth more than someone else, simply because of what you do, or who you are? Have you ever felt you weren't any more important than the next person? I was installing a telephone system at a business many years ago, and one of their customers came in, and started asking me questions about the business. I told him I was just a technician installing their new phone system. He told me, "you're never just somebody, you're just as important as anyone here". I have taken that with me, and live by that, and share that wisdom with other people. In today's reading from the Gospel of Luke, Jesus makes that same point to the Apostles. Sometimes we get so caught up in who we are, and sometimes think we deserve better, or more. We aren't necessarily any better than anyone else, and we should never treat people like they are worth less. Today, try to make every person you meet feel just as important as the next person. You will be amazed by how that changes your life as much as it changes theirs. How do you want to be treated?

Lord, may I always remember that You made every one of us, and You made each of us from Your Holy image. May I treat those I meet as I wish to be treated?

Luke 17:7-10

November 11, 2015

Are you grateful for all that you have? Do you give thanks for those who have made your life better? In this reading from the Gospel of Luke, there were ten lepers together, and they asked Jesus for mercy. Jesus healed all ten, and only one came back to Jesus and thanked him for the mercy and healing. Was he the only one that was grateful for being healed? Did the other nine want to stay as lepers, because they had something in common and could live in each other's misery, or were they just not willing to admit that Jesus had healed them? Or, did they think that it was Jesus' responsibility to heal them, and He didn't need any extra thanks? Even when people do things because they volunteered, or that's what they were meant to do, doesn't mean they don't deserve gratitude. Take time out of your day today and thank all veterans for their service. If you have the chance or the means to do it, take one out to eat, and show your gratitude for their willingness to risk their lives for people that they didn't even know. Some of them are sitting right next to you, and you may not know it. How grateful are you for what you have?

Lord, I thank You for the mercy You have given me. May You bless all of our veterans, that have given their time, and some their lives, for what they believe in.

Luke 17:11-19

November 12, 2015

Have you ever wondered when Jesus returns, if you would know it, or would you be like the Jews of Jesus' time, and still be waiting while He is already before you? When He does return, are you going to be ready? How do you know if you're ready? Do you fear His return? Will you be waiting in anticipation? I used to always wonder if I would recognize Jesus' return, or if I would be like the Jews, and be so closed minded that I wouldn't recognize the Son of Man in front of me. I know now that I will know Him when He returns. When He returns, we will see a great sign, as obvious as can be. Sometimes you wonder if the magicians, and illusionists that we see all the time are here to mess with our vision so that we don't always trust it when Jesus returns. How do you ready your heart to know Jesus when He returns? Do you have the faith to trust that You will know Him?

Lord, I trust that Your return will be so spectacular that all will know You when you come again. May You open the eyes of Your faithful to know You, even before you return.

Luke 17:20-25

November 13, 2015

How seriously do you take your salvation? Do you believe you will have a second chance after Jesus returns, and all those who have given their life to Christ have been taken up to Heaven? Where does Jesus ever talk about that? He said to them, "Where the body is, there also the vultures will gather." (Luke 17:37) Wouldn't you then assume that that body is dead, and it does not have a chance to redeem itself? We have the opportunity now to turn to Christ, and live as He has commanded us to live. When is it too late to change? When do you prepare yourself for the final judgment? I sometimes wait to do things until the last minute, but never when it is something that is important, even if it is for someone else. I don't like to make them wait, because I am not very patient myself. What is the risk, and what is the reward? We all talk like we will someday see our loved ones in Heaven one day, but are you doing anything to make that a reality? What if today was the day? Who guarantees tomorrow?

Lord, You have shown the way to Your Heavenly kingdom, may I always have my eyes on that final destination.

Luke 17:26-37

November 14, 2015

How persistent are you when you pray? Do you have a situation or person you have been praying for, and feel you haven't seen an answer? Are you praying persistently, and do you have faith that God will answer your prayer? I have a friend that has been praying for her son for many years, that he overcome his addiction, and return to his faith. She didn't expect anything to change because she had been praying for him for so long, and saw no change. I asked her if she had faith that he would change, or was she just being persistent and praying, and hoping. She said she wasn't sure she believed he would change, so she just prayed. She started praying for him, with expectant faith that he would be healed, and her life changed, and he changed his ways, and went in for treatment. He hasn't yet come back to his faith in God, at least that she is aware of, but he is on his way. Do you have faith that your prayers will be answered, and are you persistent? Do you believe your prayers will make a difference?

Lord You have answered my prayers, and I trust that You will always answer my prayers. May I always remember to bring them to You, and know that You have your own time.

Luke 18:1-8

November 15, 2015

Have you ever wondered if you will be around when the end times would happen? We see so much death and destruction that it makes us think the end is near. I think we can all look back in history, and see a time when the people of that era probably thought the end was near also. How about the people that have spent most of their lives preaching that the end is near, and then died already, before the end times. It is not something that will ever be predicted. Jesus says we will see signs, but no one knows the day or time except for the Father. We can be reassured that when the Son of Man comes, we will know it is Him. Are you prepared now, or are you planning on waiting until you see the signs of the last days? Have you received a guarantee that you will be here to see it? Is anyone given that guarantee? I have this feeling that I will be here for the end, but does that mean I will? Are we living in the times of the antichrist?

Lord, I have no guarantee of living until Your return, may I be always prepared for Your return, or my end on this earth.

Mark 13:24-32

November 16, 2015

How well do you see? Do you need glasses to see? Why is it that vision is so important that we pay so much money to be able to see better? What if you had to pay to have more faith, to see as God wants us to see, would you pay for that? Some do pay for classes to help them see God's ways better. Is your faith vision important to you? The blind man in Luke's Gospel couldn't see, and when he called out for Jesus to heal him, the crowd tried to silence him, but he cried out all the more, until Jesus healed him. It took faith to know that Jesus could heal him, but Jesus gave him a vision of faith to go with his physical sight. He immediately got up and followed Jesus. He knew why he was healed, and he knew he now had purpose, so he started to see with God's eyes. Do you call out to God to see as He sees? Do you want to see what God sees? Isn't that the vision we should all seek?

Lord God, help me to see as You see, that I may be Your hands and feet as well.

Luke 18:35-43

November 17, 2015

How far will you go to find Jesus, and purpose for your life? Zacchaeus was not very tall, a tax collector, and not a well-liked person, but he was not afraid to let people see that he also needed Jesus in his life. His life changed after finding Jesus. Jesus asked to spend some time with Him, and after Zacchaeus did spend time with Jesus, he decided to change his life, and give away half of everything he had, and even pay back those he had wronged, and stole from. In a very short time, spent with Jesus, Zacchaeus found out that the way he was living his life did not bring happiness, or purpose, so he found happiness in giving. Do you let Jesus bring out the best in you? Is Jesus enough that you can live with less? How much more joy is there in giving than in receiving? Are you willing to go out on a limb, and let people know you have found Jesus, or are searching for Him?

Lord, may I never fear what people may think of who I am, or who I serve. May my life be fulfilled with Your giving heart.

Luke 19:1-10

November 18, 2015

Do you know what your gift, or gifts are from God? Everybody has at least one, and some have more, but do you know what it is, and do you use it. I try to use my gifts daily, for fear of losing them. I know I have been given the gift of speech, the gift of writing, and the gift of persistence. It isn't always just whether you know what the gifts are, so much as, do you use them, and what do you use them for? I could use my gifts to make a lot of money, in sales, and that is how I realized my gifts, but does that please God, or give me true happiness? I can be persuasive, which can help you sell things, but it can also help you to bring people to God's Kingdom. It seems the better you get at something, the more responsibility you are given. Isn't that what Jesus' parable about the king and the ten servants is about? Didn't the king give the extra coin to the servant that doubled the coins? Do we fear the responsibility of having to do more? Is that why so many people never really use their gifts? What gifts can you share with the world, and with those around you? Do you put them to work, or do you bury them in the ground for fear of losing them?

Lord, thank You for providing me the gifts You have so graciously given me. May I be ever mindful of them, and use them to bring You glory.

Luke 19:11-28

November 19, 2015

How far are you willing to go to defend your faith, and stand up for those who believe as you believe? When Jesus says, "If you only knew what makes for peace, and the days are coming when your enemies will rise against you, and smash you", do you think He was only talking to His disciples, or was He speaking to all the generations to come? We, as Christians have been relatively free of persecution in this country, because we were founded on Christian principles. But as most of you know, we have seen an uprising of Christian persecutions in the world and the attacks have begun on Christians in this country, not so much violently, as it is suttle. When we stand by and watch it happen in other countries, we feel we can do nothing about it, but then it comes to our own doorsteps, and we have to choose. How far will you go to defend your faith? Do you stand up to those who criticize what you believe, or do you walk away, so they can attack the next Christian. Are you willing to die, as the Apostles did, for your Christian faith? Will you ever be challenged to that end? What will you do?

My God, and my Father, may I always stand with You, and never fear those that persecute me because I follow Your Son, Jesus Christ.

Luke 19:41-44

November 20, 2015

How often does your prayer include praise for God? So many times we bring our wants and needs to God, but we don't take time to praise Him. Does He need praise? Were we made in His image? Have you ever desired the praise of those you work for, or those that you supervise? How about your own children? Whenever my girls used to bring me things to fix, and I fixed them, I used to ask them, "what's my name?", and I wouldn't give it back to them until they said "Magic Man". I'm sure God doesn't need that from us, but we should still acknowledge when He has done something good in our lives. How much different are we, than God? Has He done things in Your life that have given you hope? Has He healed someone that you didn't think could be healed? Has He provided you with something you didn't think you would ever have, or deserve? Has He healed you from your ills or addictions? Doesn't God deserve the praise for all we have?

Lord, to You be the Glory, for all that I have, and for bring me the family that has been such a blessing in my life! Thank You, for all that I have.

1 Chronicles 29:10b - 12d

November 21, 2015

Do you live with the hope of the resurrection? A long time ago, one of our priests was explaining the difference between the Pharisees and the Sadducees. He said that the Sadducees don't believe in the resurrection after death, that's why they're "sad you see". That stuck with me, and helps me to remember the difference. I have many friends, as well as a parent who had remarried. The Sadducees brought a good question to Jesus. Jesus replied with the answer that, there is no marriage in Heaven. Wouldn't everyone be like those we love the most, when we enter Heaven? Don't we want it to be a place where everyone loves each other, the way we love our own family members? Who really is our brothers and our sisters? Isn't loving those we come in contact with here on earth, the way God wants us to love our family? Is your life lived with the hope of the resurrection, or is your life lived with the end being when you die here on earth, you become part of the earth? How do you find purpose in living to become part of the earth?

Lord, thank You for the promise of Heaven, and for sending Your Son, Jesus Christ, to redeem us of our sins, and give us hope of the resurrection.

Luke 20:27-40

November 22, 2015

What is your vision of a king? When you think of a king, do you think of the Henry the VIII type of king, or the David that slayed Goliath type of king? Both probably had many good traits, but both also had some bad traits. Henry the VIII liked women so much that when he lusted after one, he killed his existing wife. David had an affair, and tried to cover it up by having the leader of his army, and husband of the woman he had an affair with, moved to the front of the battle to die. Today we celebrate Jesus Christ as King. He is a different type of king than we normally think of. He is a king that sacrificed His life so that we may have eternal life, and be forgiven of our sins. When a king thinks of his servants so much that He would sacrifice His life, we don't always understand it, but doesn't a king lead us, whether into battle, or in what we should do? Isn't that the king that we all need? Someone that leads by example? Who is your king, and would you follow Him to the end?

Lord Jesus Christ, my Lord and my King, may I always be willing to serve You.

John 18:33b-37

November 23, 2015

What does Jesus see when He looks at you? Does He see someone who is giving everything to serve God, or does He see someone who tried to do just enough? What do you do daily to serve God? When is the last time you shared your faith with someone? When is the last time you held a door for someone, or offered to get something for someone that did nothing for you? Do you serve as a response to what you have received, or do you serve because it will make someone's life better? When you stop and have to wait for someone to hold the door for them, most people will say, "you didn't have to wait for me", but they usually smile and say thank you. When you share your faith, people will ask you for your help or your opinion, but are you willing to offer it? Do you offer all that you have, or just enough to get noticed by other people? Who are you serving?

Lord may I give without expecting something in return, and from my everything, and not just my excess.

Luke 21:1-4

November 24, 2015

What, in your life, would you least like to have destroyed? What is your earthly treasure? The Jews loved their temple, and all that was in it, and Jesus told them that it would be destroyed, and that would start the end times. That temple was destroyed by the Romans in 70 AD, and yet the world still exists. Does that mean that Jesus didn't know what He was talking about? What is time to God? Does God have time, as we know time? We base everything on time, yet God does not have to deal with time. God first revealed to Adam and Eve that He would return again in the book of Genesis, (Gen 3:15) yet it was thousands of years, in our time, before He sent Jesus Christ. Because we use time for everything, we don't understand why Jesus has not returned, the second time. Jesus continues to say that there will be other signs, but don't get caught up in them. Shouldn't we be more concerned about when our own temple will be destroyed? Isn't our body a temple to the Holy Spirit? We never know when our earthly lives will end, yet we live like we will stand forever, and we all know that isn't true. Have you given your life to Christ, and stopped worrying about the end? Do you fear the destruction of your temple, or do you welcome Jesus' coming with open arms?

Lord Jesus Christ, May I always be ready for your return, and not fear the loss of those things or people that may go before me?

Luke 21:5-11

Random

When you're alone with yourself, whether on the road, or walking, or just at home, do you spend that time with your own thoughts, and with God, or do you have to have a book, or some music or other noise? Why are we so afraid of quiet and being alone? I think it's interesting that in C.S. Lewis' book The Screwtape Letters, the part that Satan wants least is for us to be alone with God and our thoughts. Try turning off the noise for a while today.

November 25, 2015

Have you ever wondered why Christians are persecuted, and then we see Satan glorified in movies and on TV? I see there is a new show coming out called Lucifer and they do everything in the advertising to make him seem glamorous. Is it because it pushes the envelope, and people will tune in to see if it is good or bad? What if there was a show called Jesus, would they do the same to make Jesus look glamorous? There is a persecution that happens, and sometimes it is subtle, but other times Christians are made to look weak. In today's reading from the Gospel of Luke, Jesus tells the disciples that they will be persecuted because of Him, but He also tells them not to worry when they are questioned about what they believe. He says He will provide the words for their defense. Have you ever been confronted about your faith? Do you pause before your response, to know that God is providing you the words needed, through the Holy Spirit? Do you trust He will do that for you? What would make you not trust Jesus' words?

Lord, I trust You will give the words needed when defending the faith You have so graciously granted me. May I do my part, and trust that You will be there with me.

Luke 21:12-19

November 26, 2015

How does your faith effect those around you? Is your faith contagious, and does it change people? Today's reading from the book of Daniel is long, but it is the story of Daniel in the lion's den. Daniel's faith was strong enough to save him from the sure death of lions, and it changed a king that wanted people to have faith in nothing but him. He wanted to be the people's only hope, and prayer. Daniel spent his time in the lion's den praying and praising God, and God returned, in kind, Daniel's life, and saved him from the lions. Is your faith the kind of faith that changes people, or is it your own, to share only with God? Today when you are with family and friends, make sure to remember all that you are thankful for, and praise God for his mercy. Happy Thanksgiving! May God's many blessings be with you and your family today, and every day!

Lord, I am thankful for family and friends, and for the ability to touch lives with Your Holy and Powerful Word. To You be the Glory!

Daniel 6:12-28

November 27, 2015

Why is the fig tree used in Jesus' parables of His return? A fig tree actually produces fruit twice in a year. It produces fruit in early spring and again in the fall. Is the coming of Jesus going to be in two stages? Is Jesus' first coming, with death and resurrection the first, and His return the second, or was the fig tree used, because they were common in the region Jesus lived? There are a lot of questions about when Jesus returns, and no one will know that day or hour. Jesus tells us to watch for the signs, but more importantly He wants us to be prepared for whenever He returns. Most people start preparing for Christmas after Thanksgiving, and start shopping for gifts. Do you spend as much time and effort into preparing yourself for Jesus' return? I'm not trying to be a buzz kill, but think about how much time and money we spend on preparing for our Christmas celebration. Do you spend the same amount of effort into preparing for your final destination? What do you do to prepare your soul for Jesus' return, or for the potential untimely death? Are you still waiting for a sign? What if you die before Jesus comes the second time, are you ready for that?

Lord may I spend as much effort preparing my soul for Your return, as I do for the celebration of Your birth, and coming to earth for our redemption.

Luke 21:29-33

November 28, 2015

What will it be like when Jesus comes again, if we are still here? What if our day's end, before that time, what will it be like to stand before Jesus? One of my favorite songs is from Mercyme, called, "I can only Imagine". The lyrics are beautiful. If you have the means, search for it, and listen to the words. Here is a snip of the lyrics.

> Surrounded by Your Glory, what will my heart feel
> Will I dance for you, Jesus or in awe of You, be still
> Will I stand in Your presence, or to my knees will I fall
> Will I sing 'Hallelujah? Will I be able to speak at all?
> I can only imagine! Yeah! I can only imagine

Luke 21:34-36

November 29, 2015

Do you make New Year resolutions every year? Are they always the same, or are they different? Today is the first day of the church new year. It is the first Sunday of Advent. This is the time of year we start preparing our hearts for the coming of Christ the King, in the form of an infant. This is the time of the year we start looking at our lives and, prepare ourselves for what we need to change in our lives to ready ourselves to meet the new king. What in your life do you need to do better? Is your soul and heart ready to meet Jesus face to face? We cannot stop what will eventually happen, and it does not just affect the Christians and those that fear God. For that day will assault everyone. What kind of resolution do you need to make to change your heart, and prepare your soul? Will you be able to stand and raise your head, knowing that your redemption is at hand?

Lord, may I see with Your eyes, that I may know You, and ready my heart and my soul for Your coming.

Luke 21:25-28, 34-36

November 30, 2015

How likely are you to follow, when someone calls you to follow? When you were young and your mother or father called you, you came with no questions asked. Was that because you trusted them, and knew that you had nothing to fear, when you followed them? Do we fear following Jesus when He calls us? Why is that? Is it because of the unknown, or do we worry that others will see us following Him? Did you ever fear following a parent when they called you? Most likely not, because they were your parent, and everyone expects you to follow your parent, and people would think you were disrespectful if you didn't follow them when they called. Why do we try to ignore God's call to follow Him? Do we think He is only asking a chosen few to follow Him? Doesn't God call all of us to follow Him, as Jesus called the Apostles to follow Him? Notice that the Apostles didn't even hesitate to follow Jesus, they just got up and left everything behind, even their father. They trusted Him to lead them where they needed to go. What if you actually saw Jesus' face, and heard His voice, would you follow Him then, or would you doubt it was really Him calling you to follow?

Lord, may I always know You when You call, and be always willing to follow You, no questions asked.

Matt 4:18-22

December 2, 2015

Have you ever wondered, when you read about the feeding of the large crowds in the desert, why there is extra left over, and not just a little, but seven times as much as they started with? Some people will say that it was because the people carried their food with them and shared it with the rest of the people. Would that be a miracle, and worthy of being added into the Bible? They were in the desert three days, and Jesus was concerned they would be getting hungry, so most likely, they were not planning for that amount of time. Who carries around that much food? Sure it could show the goodness of the people that followed Jesus, and that they were paying attention to Jesus' teachings, but that wouldn't be considered a miracle. There is always more than the amount they started with. When God gives, He gives more than is needed. Even when we were young and had three little girls, and very little money, God provided for us, and more than once, people brought food to our home, in excess of what we needed. Have you experienced the giving grace of God, in your time of need? What if we never gave, and only expected God to give? Would God be as generous? Does He give to those who never give? Does He ever ask, "What have you done for me?"

Lord thank You for having such a giving heart, being always willing to provide for us. Thank You for your abundance!

Matt 15:29-37

December 3, 2015

Do you read scripture daily, or at least read these reflections daily? How often do you make it to church? Has any of it inspired you to do more for your family, friends, or community? Have you made any significant changes, or started doing things with what God has opened your eyes to? Do you really have to do anything with what you have learned? Some will say, you only need to proclaim Jesus Christ with your lips and you are saved, but is that what Jesus said? This reading from the Gospel of Matthew seems to contradict that saying. If you don't do God's will, have you really committed your life to Christ? I have a lot of friends that will argue different parts of the Bible against this teaching, but aren't the Gospels the life of Christ, and His teachings? Is there contradiction in the Bible? If we used the Bible to point out the flaws of other Christians, are we really doing God's will? Aren't there enough people trying to destroy Christianity, that we don't need to go after each other? What have you done to build your foundation, and make sure you can withstand the storms that are sure to come your way? Have you built your faith life on the rock that is Jesus Christ, by doing what He asks you to do, or are you just going to watch and see what happens?

Lord, may I always remember that You paid a price for my soul, and You deserve for me to make an effort to do the same for others.

Matthew 7:21, 24-27

December 4, 2015

How strong is your faith? When you ask God for healing, or something specific, do you believe God is capable of making it happen? What if God said to you, "let it be done for you according to your faith"? Would your faith allow for the healing? Is that why we don't always see the healing, we ask for, or that one thing that we think will be what we need? Do you believe God is capable of that kind of healing? Jesus asked the two blind men if they believed in Him, and that He could heal them, and after they said, "Yes, Lord", Jesus said, "let it be done according to your faith". (Matthew 9:29) Do you have faith enough to bring about healing, and if you don't, what is stopping you from believing? Is it doubt, or skepticism, or is it because you have never witnessed a miracle?

Lord, when my faith is weak, show me things that help me believe, and when I have doubt, grant me Your grace to see.

Matt 9:27-31

December 5, 2015

Are you part of the harvest, or are you one of the laborers sent to collect the harvest? If you are one of the laborers, most likely you were part of the harvest at one time. How do you know which one you are? If you are talking to somebody, and you have the opportunity to share your faith with them, and how Jesus' life and death and resurrection has changed your life, then you are a laborer at that time. Sometimes we are the harvest, and sometimes the laborers. No matter which you are, you are to do this with no cost, because Jesus did not charge us for what He did. He only asks that we share what we have received with those we meet. He doesn't give it as an option, He sends out the disciples and gives them authority over unclean spirits. Do you feel you have the power to make that kind of difference, and be the one who goes to the world and delivers God's message, and helps to change the world? If not us, then who should do it?

Lord, with Your help and guidance I am able to do Your work, and help with the harvest. May I go where You send me.

Matt 9:35–10:1, 5a, 6-8

December 6, 2015

How often do you pray for those you meet each and every day? How about those you have only met once or twice? Do you pray for those who lead you to a better life in knowing God more deeply? Did you know that most priests and pastors pray for the people in their parish and congregation? How often have you prayed for them? They need your prayer more than most, because they have to constantly do battle with their own demons to carry on. Satan is real, and sometimes it seems like the closer you try to be with God, and doing His work, the more Satan will try to disrupt you. Those who lead us in our spiritual life, need our prayers for strength, and encouragement to keep pressing on. I have a lot better understanding of the commitment of those who lead us, and greatly appreciate them for all they do. Will you offer up a prayer for all of our spiritual leaders today, and thank them the next time you see them, for all that they do?

Lord, thank you for the spiritual guidance of our priests, deacons, pastors, and all who have dedicated their lives to serving You, and giving hope to the lost. May Your loving blessings and grace be with them always.

Philippians 1:4-6, 8-11

December 7, 2015

Have you ever joined up with a group of people and prayed for someone who was in desperate need of prayer, and healing? Jesus tells us that whenever two or more are gathered in His name, He is there. So why don't we do this more often for those in need? The paralyzed man in this Gospel reading was brought to Jesus by a group of men, and Jesus forgave them of their sins, and healed the paralyzed man. He doesn't just heal the one in physical need, and brought to prayer, He also heals those that bring the person to Him. There is healing in praying for people, and changes happen to all. About twenty years ago, I attended a three day retreat that I wasn't sure I wanted to be at, but stayed none the less. I was healed along with the rest of us that were there, but at the end we were given envelopes of people that were praying for us while we were there, and nearly every man that opened and read the prayers being offered for him, wept. When is the last time you took someone to Jesus in prayer, and offered them up? Do you know that kind of healing?

Lord, thank You for the prayer warriors that spend most of their time in prayer to You, not just for themselves, but for all Your people.

Luke 5:17-26

December 8, 2015

If you were God, and decided all things, how would you bring your son into the world? Would you choose who was to be the vessel, or womb, that would carry Your Son, based on certain criteria, or would you make sure it is spotless from the start? If you were to choose who would carry Your Son, and savior of the world, would you also make sure, from the start of that woman's life, that she too would be pure? If you were God, wouldn't you be able to do that? There is so much contention between Christian religions over things that were not thought of to separate, but to give thought and prayer to. Because the misunderstandings of who Mary is, some Christians have negative thoughts towards all who believe Mary is someone special. The Angel Gabriel came to Mary, and said, "Hail, full of grace! The Lord is with you."(Luke 1:28) He never asked Mary to carry Jesus, the Son of God, he just told her that she is. God had already prepared her, and Gabriel was sent to tell her what to expect. Mary accepted God's call, and carried His Son, as her own son, as all mothers would carry and care for their children. Is Mary just another person God has called to serve, or is she someone God has chosen, and made as the mother of His Son Jesus Christ? If you believe Mary is something more, does that make you a bad Christian?

Lord, may You help with the understanding of why Mary was chosen, and why so many people deny her importance in bringing Jesus into this world? Let us say, as the angel Gabriel said, "Hail Mary! Full of grace, the Lord is with you."

Luke 1:26-38

December 9, 2015

Have you ever gotten to a place where you felt you just couldn't go on anymore? Do you get to that place and just want to throw in the towel because it all seems to be too much? Most of the time we get to our desperate spot before we finally call on God to pull us through. Why is that? Is it because we feel we should be able to do this on our own? We really don't need any help? Why are we so afraid of asking God for help in everything we do? Are we worried He will become tired of hearing from us and ignore us? God never gets weary. He never gets to the place where He wants to give up on us, no matter how much we ask for His help. When we seek God for help, He gives us the strength to to keep going. Think about when Jesus was going through the crucifixion, and kept going, even knowing that what was at the end of that long road, carrying a cross. He still kept going when most people would have said, "you're going to kill me anyway, and I'm not going to carry this cross anymore!" God gives us the strength, no matter how often we call on Him. Will you call on God to be your strength, and help you through the times when you feel like giving up?

Lord, so many times I feel this is my battle, and my foolish pride makes me want to do this on my own. May I always remember that You are always there to carry me, no matter the condition.

Isaiah 40:25-31

December 10, 2015

What is the reason for the violence in this world? Is it because of God? Why do people say that religion is the cause of all wars? God has never promoted killing, yet people attribute their wars and violence to God. We see people that go to the extremes, and believe they are killing for God, but did God really cause them to act the way they did? When Jesus was on earth, He was abused physically, but did He ever strike back? The closest thing He did to violence was turning over the tables of the money changers that were disgracing God's temple. If ever there was a time for violence, Jesus would have been justified to fight back when He was being crucified. John the Baptist came to announce the coming of the Savior of the world, and he was imprisoned, and later killed because of it. The Apostles were killed because they were proclaiming Jesus Christ, yet none of them fought back. Were they the cause of the violence? No, they were the result of what happens to people that are strong in their faith, and believe differently. Why is God the one that is under attack? Does He start the wars and killing? Isn't it more the misguided people that use God as a reason, for their violence?

Lord, we have seen your mercy, and we know the love You provide, by seeing what Jesus has done for us, may we know your love, and share that same love with those we meet.

Matt 11:11-15

December 11, 2015

What if we did everything that God had taught us to do? What if we were always truthful? What if we never tried to control whether or not we had children, or a certain number of children? What if everything we did was for God? What would be different about your life? How many families do you know that had a dozen or more children? Did they survive? Did they learn to make it with what they had? I'm not saying we should all have a dozen or more kids, we chose how many we had, I'm only saying that God never intended us to be in control of the number of children we had. Do we always trust God to provide for us? If we do, why do we control something like the number of children we have? Does that say we don't trust God? What about our integrity? Can we be trusted in everything we are involved in? Why was Jesus sent to us? Because we are not always capable of doing all that God asks of us. God provided us His Son, to forgive us our sins, because we are human, and not Devine. We make mistakes, and sometimes just bad judgement. What will you do to try to be more of who God created you to be? Will you pray more for guidance, and trust what God asks of you?

Lord, please forgive me for the times I have not trusted You, and made decisions based on my wants, and not Yours. May I be ever aware of what You ask of me, and do your will.

Isaiah 48:17-19

December 13, 2015

Have you been baptized? Have you been confirmed in the Holy Spirit? Are they two separate things? In the Catholic Church, these are two completely separate sacraments. Baptism is for the forgiveness of original sin, and Confirmation is a declaration by the recipient that they are willing to follow Jesus, and are sealed in the Holy Spirit. The Holy Spirit is a gift from Jesus to walk in His path, and a guide to help us in Jesus' path. When we are young, we are nearly always with our parents and we feel secure. Baptism is a sacrament to know that we have been washed away of original sin. When we get older, we have the opportunity to leave our parents and go it alone, and make decisions on our own. Confirmation is giving us the guide to help us in our journey, and to be there to help us do the right thing, and say the right thing. Do you let the Holy Spirit guide you in your journey on this earth?

Lord thank You for the gift of Baptism and the gift of Confirmation. May You always guide me, and may I always follow.

Luke 3:10-18

December 14, 2015

Why do people let their pride put them into positions they cannot get out of? The chief priests and elders were trying to trap Jesus, and Jesus set a trap for them instead. They were trying to get Him to say His power came from Heaven, so they could have Him arrested for blasphemy. They had heard John the Baptist speak and knew that the people believed John was Elijah returned, and they still had him arrested, because John was teaching differently than they were teaching. They taught with authority and control, with laws that were nearly impossible to live by, and John taught with authority and compassion. When someone confronts you about your faith in God, and Jesus Christ as your savior, do you trust that the Holy Spirit will guide your words? Was Jesus' words guided by the Holy Spirit? Doesn't God, Jesus, and the Holy Spirit make up the Holy Trinity? If Jesus relied on the Holy Spirit, why wouldn't we be able to also rely on Him when we need the words to say? Didn't the Holy Spirit get sent when Jesus ascended into Heaven? Why do we fear having the right words to say, when we are speaking of God? Do you have that kind of faith?

Lord God and Father, may I always trust that You will provide my words, and guide my thoughts, that I may never lead Your children astray.

Matthew 21:23-27

December 15, 2015

What would God have to do in your life to make you do His will? Is there something He could do to change you, and make you want to do as He asks? If God has done a great work in you, have you done anything to show your thankfulness? Some will say that they don't have to go to church on the weekend, because they find God in their daily lives, but what about the person that doesn't see God as you do, and needs to make it to church to find new life? Do we need to live by example so others may see that? When God asks you to do something, do you do it with a grateful heart, or do you say you will, and then don't do it? Do we have to do what God asks us to do? Some will say works are not part of what God asks of us, but then how do you show God your love for Him? How do you show your parents and family that you love them? Do you show them by doing, or do you just tell them?

Lord, may my actions be a sign of my love for You, and may my yes be a yes of doing, not just in word.

Matthew 21:28-32

December 16, 2015

How well do you know the people around you? Do you have friends that do things, away from the life you see them in that you never expected them to do? Do you know your friends and family members like God knows them? John the Baptist's purpose in his time on earth was to proclaim the coming of the Messiah. He baptized Jesus in the Jordan River, and saw the Spirit of God come down on Him, and say, "This is my Son in whom I am well pleased". So why did John send two of his disciples to ask Jesus if He is the one they are looking for? Did John want them to stop following him, so they would start to follow the Messiah? Wouldn't John's disciples have gone if he would have told them that they need to start following Jesus? Was Jesus more than even John was expecting Him to be? When we know someone, and we think we really know them, God will occasionally open our eyes to see them in a different light. Sometimes you find the person you have known since your childhood, doing things that could only be from God, and you wonder if you ever really knew them at all. How well do you really know Jesus? Has He done things in Your life that you never really expected?

Lord thank You for the gift of vision, and opening my eyes to see You more clearly, and know You more personally.

Luke 7:18b-23

December 17, 2015

Have you ever done your family genealogy? It's amazing some of the things you find out, when you look back on history. We all have good history, and we all have bad, even Jesus' family history has some bumps in the road. Judah had twins with his daughter in-law. David (King David, of David and Goliath fame) lusted over his battle commander's wife Bathsheba, and couldn't resist temptation, so he had her brought to his castle and she became pregnant with Solomon. So David called Uriah back so he would sleep with his wife and cover his own sin, but Uriah was so loyal to David that he wanted to get back to battle for his king, and wouldn't even spend time with Bathsheba. So what does David do to cover his sin, he sends Uriah to the front of the battle to get killed. Yes we all have some dark history. David was so repentant of his sins that he wrote most of the book of Psalms. He did a great thing for God, and everyone that has come since, and wishes to praise God. Have you looked into your past? Have you done anything to show your repentant spirit?

Lord You know my past, and you know my future, may I serve You in all that I do, that You may be glorified.

Matthew 1:1-17

December 18, 2015

How strong is you faith? When you hear or see something while in prayer, do you truly believe it, even if it means you could be ridiculed for that belief? So Joseph was a righteous man, and he wasn't married yet to Mary, and in those days, an unmarried pregnant girl was chastised and ridiculed, along with the father. Yet Joseph heard in a dream, or prayer, that his soon to be wife was pregnant, and he wasn't the father, and he was to take her into his house. There, is extreme faith, or knowing that what you heard in prayer is what you believe. Do you tell all your friends and family that story? Why would they believe it? Was there a different kind of faith in that time? What if you told that same story about your future wife today, how many people would believe you? Does it matter if they believe you? Did Joseph have more faith then we do, or did he just trust his dreams/prayers that much? How much faith do you have in what you hear in prayer? Is it enough to face that kind of ridicule, and not fear other people?

Lord, I trust You with my everything, and all of who You have made me. May I be as convicted, and as trusting in what You show me during prayer, as Joseph and Mary.

Matthew 1:18-25

December 19, 2015

Have you prayed a long time for something, and when the prayer is answered, couldn't believe it? This reading from the Gospel of Luke is the story of Zechariah and Elizabeth, the parents of John the Baptist. They had been praying for a baby for many years, and when the Angel Gabriel came to Zechariah in prayer, to tell him that his wife will bear them a son, Zechariah didn't believe it, so his punishment was to not be able to speak. Yesterday we saw Joseph do things most people would not do, and today we see disbelief in what we hear in prayer. Do you always believe what you hear in prayer? Do you trust that God can speak to you, and does, while in prayer? Why do we still not trust our prayers, and answers?

My God, and my Father may I always trust that You can and will speak to me, and be confident that it is You, and trust that You will do as You say.

Luke 1:5-25

December 20, 2015

What is your sign from God, that points to Jesus Christ? The last couple of days we see how different people respond to what they hear in prayer. Joseph said, "Yes", and Zechariah said, "Really?"(my interpretation) Today we see Mary come to Elizabeth, Zechariah's wife, and mother of John the Baptist, and John does what he was put here to do, announce the presence of the Messiah. Have you ever wondered why this part about Mary visiting Elizabeth was in the Bible? What is it trying to say? Is it God showing us that, even in the womb, people are important? Why do so many people think that the baby in the womb has no purpose, until they are outside the womb? Didn't John announce the presence of God in the room, from the womb? Didn't Jesus start changing lives from inside the womb? Was this reading to show that God has already provided His Holy Spirit for these two special people, and the babies in their wombs? God doesn't tell us stories just to fill dead space on a page, He provides them to help us understand other things that are taking place, or that are to take place. Do you recognize God when you see Him, or hear His voice, or see a sign?

Lord, to know You has changed my life, may I have the strength and courage to show those I come in contact with, how You can change lives.

Luke 1:39-45

December 21, 2015

Are you anxiously awaiting this Christmas season, like a child awaits the opening of the presents? Christmas is a special time of year, because we celebrate the coming of our Savior. When you give a gift for a birthday or Christmas don't you also receive the joy of seeing the person opening the gift, with excitement and anticipation? The best part about Christmas is we receive the gift of salvation through Jesus' coming and dying on the cross. God has given us a gift, and wants to know our joy in receiving the gift He has freely given us. Will you show God your thankfulness for His giving this Christmas season? Will you recall the gift given for all, and be thankful? Will you sing with joy in your heart?

Lord may I always be joyfully singing Your praises, all throughout the year. Thank You for the gift of Your Son.

Zephaniah 3:14-18a

December 22, 2015

Are you strengthened by knowing Jesus Christ? Has God empowered you to fight with Him, in the battle of good and evil? Did God send His Son to save our souls from the fiery eternity, and that is all we should be concerned about? Mary speaks of God's mighty plan for the battle of our souls. In the world we live in, there is always a battle for who we are, and who we can be. If Satan wasn't a threat to our souls, would God need to send His Son? Yes we create our own trouble, but is that us alone, or are we persuaded by evil? Have you made it a point to expose the evil that exists in this world, or do you sit back and think it will go away by itself? What have you done to change the souls of those around you? We all know the person in our life that needs to know that God exists, and Jesus is the answer to saving their soul, but what have you done to help them see what you have seen? Is that person worth as much as you are? Do they know the joy of the same Christmas you know?

Lord may I be always aware of those that are searching for You, and don't know it yet, so that they may hear Your saving story.

Luke 1:46-56

December 23, 2015

Have you ever been speechless, because of something the Lord has revealed to you? Zechariah was left speechless because he didn't believe the Angel Gabriel when he was told his wife Elizabeth was to conceive a child that would be dedicated to God, and would have the purpose of announcing the arrival of the Messiah. Doesn't God want all of us to be John the Baptist? Doesn't He want us all to take that roll, and proclaim the coming of the Messiah? How many people do you come in contact with each day? Of all those people, how often do you talk about who Jesus is, and what He has done in your life? Do you tell them that Jesus will come again? Is it because it wasn't the right place or time? When is that time? Do you talk to people about the weather, or sports, or a movie, or a TV show, or politics? We can always make time to talk about things that mean very little in our purpose here, yet we can't find the right opportunity to speak about what can change their salvation. Why are we left speechless when it comes to speaking about God? It may not be politically correct to do it, but if it was something you were passionate about, would you care if it was politically correct? What will it take for you to get your voice back to speak about who God is in your life?

Lord, may I make it a point to speak to people today about the life that awaits those who have accepted Your Son Jesus Christ. May You provide the strength and the words to speak of Your loving Grace.

Luke 1:57-66

December 24, 2015

Are you ready for Jesus to come into your heart to live? The Jewish people were waiting for years for the Messiah to come, and before Him would be the one calling out in the desert, John the Baptist. After months of silence, Zechariah was speaking, and proclaiming what his son was to do. What are your memories of Christmases past? Like most kids, we couldn't wait for Christmas, and our parents never put our presents under the tree until Christmas Eve, so we were always looking to find their hiding place. Every once in a while we found them, hiding in the trunk of the car, in their bedroom closet, or under their bed. We were not patient, so we even tried to figure out who was getting what. One Christmas we got up right after mom and dad went to bed, and opened our gifts before they got up. Needless to say, they were not happy. Are you giddy with anticipation for this Christmas? Will you let others know your joy in Christ's coming? Christmas isn't about us, it's about what God has done for us, and we should always be thankful for that special gift.

Lord, be our welcome guest this Christmas, that we may know You and be receptive of Your special gift.

Luke 1:67-79

December 25, 2015

What is the greatest gift you have ever received? This is not a trick question. Even when we were children, and raced out to see what we were given for Christmas, we probably could never imagine a gift so great, as a gift from God. To those of you who knew God's gift from childhood, were you ever fully able to explain it to those that didn't know? We have received a great gift, and we should want to share it with everyone we meet. How will you show others the gift God has poured out for you?

My God, and my Lord, may my heart always know the love in Your gift freely given to the world.

May God's blessings be with you now and always? Wishing you a Merry Christmas from our family! Thank you also, to all of you who take the time out of your day to read these reflections. My prayer is that God can use a simple person like myself to show the love He has for each of us. Have a Blessed Christmas!

Luke 2: 1-14

December 26, 2015

Why do we celebrate Jesus' birth with such rejoicing? We welcome Jesus into the world to give us new life, but what does He truly bring to us in this life? Many people have asked why I focus so much on being bold, and going out and proclaiming our salvation through Jesus Christ. Isn't that what Jesus truly came here for? Yes, He came to provide a path for us to Heaven through His sacrifice on the cross, but He knew that could cost us our life on this earth the same as it cost Him, His life. Today we recognize Stephen as the first martyr for Jesus, after His death and resurrection. Why is this the day after Christmas? Jesus said "Beware of men, for they will hand you over to courts and scourge you in their synagogues, and you will be led before governors and kings for my sake as a witness before them and the pagans. (Matthew 10:17) Stephen spoke boldly, and was killed for what God wanted him to say, because he believed what Jesus preached, and boldly proclaimed it, knowing it could cost him his life. When you think about the birth of Jesus in the manger, do you also think about why He came, and what He did for you, and what He is calling you to do? Will you boldly go where Jesus, and so many before us, have gone, and know that the Holy Spirit will guide you?

Jesus, thank you for coming with the simplicity that You entered the world, and strength that You provide through the guidance of Your Holy Spirit.

Acts 6:8-10; 7:54-59

December 27, 2015

Do you teach your children about your faith in God, and what it means to be a follower of Christ? We hear all these new terms for parents, and the way they raise them. There are helicopter parents, and free range kids. New young parents are always learning. Think about the way you were raised. We would have been considered free range kids, probably like most kids that were raised before the new millennium. We ran with the neighbor kids and needed to be home when the street lights came on. That doesn't mean our parents didn't love us, it just means they trusted we would do as they said. Jesus was raised as a free range child. Notice in this reading from the Gospel of Luke that Mary and Joseph were looking for Him among their caravan for a day, and when they found Jesus, it had been three days. They had raised Jesus the way all good parents raised their kids, by teaching them to respect their parents and to know the Jewish traditions and laws. Usually be age twelve they had memorized the first five books of the Bible. Have you spent enough time in the Bible to have memorized any of it, much less teach your kids to do it? When our children learn to follow Christ, and understand a true love for God, they also see a true love for them, by the way parents live their lives. How will you show God to your children, and family members?

Lord, thank You for the gift of family, and showing us how to love You through a loving caring family.

Luke 2: 41-52

December 28, 2015

Do you acknowledge that you are a sinner, even though you are a Christian? Just because you are a Christian, does that mean you no longer sin? Do you still have anger? Do you still have jealousy? Do you still have pride? Of course you do. The difference is that now you acknowledge that you are a sinner, and you also have forgiveness of those sins. Does that mean you are now free to sin all you want, as long as you ask forgiveness? No, it just means you acknowledge that you will still sin, and you will ask for forgiveness and try not to repeat your sin. If you continue to do the same sin, and then ask forgiveness of that sin, are you truly repenting of your sin, or just using it for an excuse to sin more? The difference between Christians and non-Christians is that we acknowledge we are sinners and have the same Jesus Christ that died for their sins as well as ours, who has died for our sins. Do you acknowledge your sinful ways? Do you seek forgiveness for your sins?

Lord please forgive me of my sinfulness, and help me to be the man You have called me to be.

1 John 1:5 - 2:2

December 29, 2015

What in your life gives you purpose? Have you ever said, "If you allow me to see this one thing, or experience that one thing, I would die happy."? It seems we all have something that we want to experience before we die, but I can't say that I am looking forward to one specific thing, and ready to die right after. Simeon was a Holy Religious man, who spent a lot of time in prayer, so much so that the Holy Spirit was with him, even before God sent Him to the people at Pentecost. He recognized that Jesus is the Christ child that was foretold to him. Simeon was allowed to see that one thing that God had promised to him, and the Holy Spirit revealed to him. Do you pray for that kind of vision? Have you asked the Holy Spirit to reveal to you the life changing thing that shows God's plan for you? Some people don't want to know it, because they don't know if they can live that kind of life. What is "that kind of life" that we would fear it, or not want to live it, if God showed it to us? Have you prayed for the Holy Spirit to give you vision? Will you be obedient if it is revealed to you?

Lord, I want to see with Your eyes, that I may know the plans You have for me, and that I may see as You want me to see. May Your Holy Spirit guide my heart?

Luke 2: 22-35

December 30, 2015

How much do you love the world you live in? Have you ever compared that love to the love you have for God? Do you love God more than this world? We hear so often of people who want to save the world and all that is in it, and they want us to change our way of living to save the world, but do they love the Lord? Which is more important? Can you do both? Yes you can, as long as your priorities are kept in check. There are so many things in this world that are distracting. Think about the time you are on Facebook, and the range of things you see. You see moments of joy, moments of loss, people asking for prayer, people sharing things that you would not want your children to see, and occasionally uplifting messages, and encouragement. It is no different than what we see in the world. We have the ability to choose what we care to see, and what we want to be part of. Sometimes we see things that we would rather not see, but do you stay to see more, or do you skim past, and move on? Would you risk eternity what is in the world? Do you love God more than these things of the world?

Lord, You know when I am weak, and when I feel the pull of this world, may You give me the strength to resist the things that the evil one puts before me as temptation. May my love for you, give me the strength to move on.

1 John 2:12-17

December 31, 2015

Have you ever wondered if you are living in the time of the antichrist? Have you ever wondered if you would be on earth when the final antichrist comes? There have been people in our time that seem to be an antichrist. What is an antichrist? Isn't it the one to come, to oppose Jesus Christ for the final battle of the souls of humankind? Wouldn't he also be the one to try and convince people that there is no God, and therefore no Jesus, or Holy Spirit? What would this world be like if there were no God? Doesn't all good come from God? Isn't God the source of all light, love, and all that is good? What would it be like to live in that world? The opposite is to live in Heaven, where there is no evil, no one trying to take advantage of you, no one to lie to you, no one to try and hurt you, physically, or emotionally. What would that be like? Do you know the truth? When you hear from the final antichrist that is to come, will you be able to determine the difference between Christ, and the antichrist? If you know God, and therefore truth, you will be able to see the lie. How do you ready yourself for that test? Do you spend time in God's Holy Word?

Lord, may You keep my eyes open to know You more deeply and fully, that I may know truth, and never be deceived.

1 John 2:18-21